A Thomas Jefferson Education

"TJEd" is a philosophy and a methodology by which great individuals throughout history were educated. Thousands of families and professional educators are applying those same principles today, with astounding success. This new paperback edition includes:

+ The 7 Keys of Great Teaching
+ The 4 Phases of Learning
+ The 5 Environments of Mentoring
+ Tips for professional educators
+ How to apply Thomas Jefferson Education in a homeschool
+ Teaching the classics of math, science, history, the arts, etc.
+ Thomas Jefferson Education in college and careers

"As a high school teacher and administrator, I have yearned for a different approach to learning; and Oliver DeMille shows us how education should really take place—with classics and mentors, where students must dig it out for themselves with a little guidance. It may take a whole generation to throw off the bad habits, but let's get started."

—EARL TAYLOR, PRINCIPAL
HERITAGE ACADEMY, CHARTER HIGH SCHOOL

"I felt like I was reading the *Common Sense* of the Twenty-first Century, the book that will shape the minds of the leaders."

—TIFFANY EARL, HOMESCHOOLING MOTHER,
FOUNDER OF LEADERSHIP EDUCATION METHODS INSTITUTE

"Oliver DeMille has analyzed history and brilliantly given us, as Abraham Lincoln said, 'just that knowledge of past men and events which [we] need' in our lives and schools."

—VICKI JO ANDERSON, FORMER PRESIDENT
ARIZONA CHARTER SCHOOLS ASSOCIATION

A Thomas Jefferson Education

TEACHING A GENERATION OF LEADERS
FOR THE TWENTY-FIRST CENTURY

Oliver DeMille

Note: This volume is a philosophical overview, and not a step-by-step guide for implementation of the Leadership Education model. For additional help on application, see *Leadership Education: The Phases of Learning* and the other titles in the Leadership Education Library.

The Leadership Education Library

Volume 1: *A Thomas Jefferson Education: Teaching a Generation of Leaders for the 21st Century*
Volume 2: *Leadership Education: The Phases of Learning*
Volume 3: *A Thomas Jefferson Education Home Companion*
Volume 4: *Thomas Jefferson Education for Teens*
Volume 5: *The Student Whisperer: Inspiring Genius*
Volume 6: *19 Apps: Leadership Education for College Students*

To download an index of the contents of this book, visit TJEd.org/TJEd-Index.

TJEd.org / OliverDeMille.com

First paperback edition published in 2000. First hardback edition, revised, published in 2006. Second paperback edition 2009. Third paperback edition 2012.

Inquiries regarding requests to reprint all or part of this book, or distribution or publishing questions, should be addressed to contact@tjed.org.

Thanks to Julie Earl, Michele Smith, Brad Bolon, Janine Bolon, Rachel DeMille, Tiffany Earl, Shanon Brooks, Tressa Roberts, Andrew Groft, Nels Jensen and Daniel Earley for editorial suggestions. Thanks to Shawn Ercanbrack for sections of chapter ten and the epilogue. The author is responsible for the contents of this book.

Printed in the United States of America.

Cover and book design by Daniel Ruesch Design | danielruesch.net

ICBN 978-0-9830996-6-6
LCCN 2012907883

To Van & Janice DeMille

Jefferson Mentors

*"If a nation expects to be ignorant and free,
in a state of civilization,
it expects what never was and never will be."*

—*Thomas Jefferson*

Contents

APPENDICES

To download an index of the contents of
this book, visit TJEd.org/TJEd-Index

CHAPTER ONE

Two Towers

*"Lay down true principles, and adhere to them inflexibly.
Do not be frightened into their surrender..."*

— *Thomas Jefferson*

"**O**liver, turn on the radio, now!"
There was an urgency I'd seldom heard in Dr. Brooks' voice, and he hung up without saying anything else. So I hurried to the radio and switched it on. Frankly, I am not a morning person and had failed to answer his three earlier phone calls. But on the fourth set of long rings, I finally picked it up. We didn't have a television in our home—part of a typical summer routine for our family, meant to get us all to study, talk and build relationships instead of waste our family time in front of the set. The radio told of an event that would change the world, and I immediately called Dr. Brooks back and told him to contact the student body and call a campus-wide meeting.

It was the morning of September 11, 2001.

There is a longing that perhaps we all feel in the beginning decades of the Twenty-first Century. Maybe human beings have always felt it, but something unique seems to be growing and spreading in our world today. Mediocrity, which became the norm and in some circles even the goal between 1968 and 2001, seemed to lose its hold on that tragic morning when the whole world tuned in to watch the Twin Towers fall—over and over and over. Since "9/11," we now live in a different world.

It remains to be seen what the Twenty-first Century holds in store, but we learned a few things on that morning that are valuable lessons for the future. First, every generation faces its challenges. The modern feeling of invincibility and the view that peace and prosperity are the natural state of things has been brought into question. Most of us are much more painfully aware of just how fragile our enjoyable lifestyle really is. Even the return to normalcy in the years since 9/11 only masks the new sense of vulnerability Americans now feel.

The looks on the faces of my students as I walked into the main classroom told me what a shock this really was. The questions were emotional and basic: "How long will it last?" "What can we expect in the days and even years ahead?" "What will this mean to the future of our nation?" "Are all my plans and dreams for the future gone forever?" and "What should I be doing to help?"

These young people felt something new that day, something you don't ever forget. Virtually all who experienced those feelings that morning are deeply changed. They know it could happen again, on any day at any given moment—and they live with that. Moreover, somewhere inside many people actually expect it. The youth of 9/11 are no longer living in a world of Comedy, where we all feel an underlying security that everything will turn out well. We lived through one of those junctures in history when a world of Comedy shifts to Tragedy, and with this on our minds, day after day, week after week, through each holiday season and with every new year, our souls steel with each passing month and our subconscious emotions prepare us for what is ahead. I believe we all feel it on some level—even those who deny it.

Preparing for Leadership

"What can I possibly say to these young people?" I wondered, wishing my father were present. He had served in Vietnam, and seemed to have come home with an ability to face any crisis—evenly and calmly giving brief words of wisdom that soothed and protected. My own experience hadn't prepared me for this. When the Gulf War began in 1991 I watched in technicolor in a university auditorium and discussed the evils of war with my college classmates. By 2001, the ten years since that event felt like an eternity. In fact, it was an irony that most of the George Wythe College students were supposed to discuss the book *Alas Babylon* that morning. This modern classic, set during the Cold War, opens on a morning when a nuclear war changes the face of the land and the people who survive. Clearly, reading the book wasn't anything like the reality of terrorists flying planes into buildings right now—in the real world.

I looked into the faces of the students, and wondered what to say. Fortunately, before I opened my mouth Dr. Einar Erickson stood. He probably saw me in the same light as the students: young, shell-shocked, and scared. If so, he was right.

Dr. Erickson, who had lived through Pearl Harbor, told of that time over fifty years before. By the time he finished, two things had occurred. First, I think everyone in the room was moved to tears. And second, we were calmed and anchored. Things would work out, there were a lot of decisions ahead for our generation, and there was much work to be done. As students and faculty, we could either ignore these events and escape into campus life, or we could take this head on, realize that great things are going to be asked of our generation, and set out to prepare ourselves to help fill the leadership drought around the world. Dr. Erickson said all the right things. He gave us something to do. He led.

When I got the microphone back, I was ready. "At some point in your life," I said, "you will face a situation where you are in a leadership position and dozens—maybe thousands or millions—look to you to lead. When that occurs, you won't feel ready. But you will have to lead anyway. Today, we're going to do something that in all probability isn't being done anywhere else. We're going to simulate the Situation Room at the White House today, and we're going to learn what's happening."

I assigned each student to a team led by a faculty member and told them they had thirty minutes to find out the positions and names of every person who would likely be advising the President today and to appoint a student to fill each position. Then I gave them one hour to research the person they were role-playing, and to meet back with recommendations for the President. I don't know if other groups simulated this event that day, but just like Pearl Harbor or Chamberlain's visit with Hitler, I'm sure it will be simulated by many students at many schools in the years to come. Simulation is a powerful learning tool, and that day was a sobering and life-changing experience for all who lived through it.

A second lesson of the day is that when crisis comes, we naturally turn to God. Before we broke for our research, one student raised his hand and asked if we could please pray. The room unanimously consented, and another student volunteered to say the prayer. We all felt the enormity of the task our world was facing, and more tears were shed during that prayer. People from many faiths and churches prayed that day in the United States, including many who hadn't set foot in a church for a long time. Across America, the level of religious observance increased that day.

A third lesson from 9/11 is that when crisis hits, we automatically look to leadership. As we were preparing to break into groups for research, the door opened and in walked several former students. They were no longer studying at George Wythe College, but when they first heard the news of the terrorist attacks they immediately grabbed a change of clothes, jumped in their vehicles and drove to Cedar City—one student drove five hours and arrived just as we were making plans. Of course, the whole nation looked to President Bush, just as people in other nations looked to their leaders.

In crisis, leadership determines direction and our level of success—or failure. Unfortunately, in such times it is too late to prepare leaders. They must be trained, educated, and gain the needed experience before crisis occurs. Yet it is precisely in the years and decades before crisis that peace and prosperity convince the world that such leadership is not needed—making a living takes hold of society and material goals drive schools, teachers, parents and students alike. Professional training and job skills are all that people seek from "education," and the concept of leadership education is considered quaint, outdated, frivolous, or absurd. Allan Bloom's *The Closing of the American Mind* was widely sold, but sparsely read and soundly rejected by a generation of educators. His suggestions, which would have helped prepare a generation of leaders for the Twenty-first Century, were mostly ridiculed or ignored, just as the same suggestions by Jacques Barzun had been disregarded a generation earlier and those of Adler and Hutchins a generation before that.

Perhaps in the wake of 9/11, such prophetic warnings will be more closely considered. Certainly the warning signs had been there for over a decade—terrorists were planning attacks on American soil. And in the broader context, a time is soon coming when a generation of leaders will be needed, when a society trained on the mostly narrow or otherwise deficient educational offerings that are now the norm in our nation will not be enough to overcome the challenges we face. This is the fourth lesson of 9/11, which it seems no society ever wants to learn: that we must learn from our past and heed the cycles, trends, and historical patterns that inevitably (in one form or another) repeat themselves. Santayana was right: if we don't learn the lessons of history, we are doomed to repeat them.

Is Mediocre Education Enough?

A fifth lesson is that although wisdom is usually thought to be found in the elderly, in times of challenge it is often the young who provide answers. Many of the older generations, who lived and loved and raised families and went to work every day in a world of peace and prosperity, seem fully addicted to a view that crisis is just a passing fad, that everything will quickly return to normal if we just ignore the depth of the problems. As the months after 9/11 turned into years, adult America was only too happy to go back to "business as usual," telling itself that maybe this was just a tragic one-time event that has passed and won't return. The young have no such illusion—they doubt they'll ever receive a Social Security check, and most of them are sure that serious conflicts are ahead. Naturally, they seek to prepare themselves—often bewildering their parents who wonder why they don't just focus on credentials and secure jobs. "As if any job will be secure in my world," the under-thirty crowd quips.

A sixth lesson is that the young are all about one thing: making the world better. They want to do something, not just leave it to others. And with their leadership, a surprising number of the earlier generations join in the cause. A growing cadre of people are aligning their futures with leadership. This is not the "electronic herd" of 1980s yuppie fame or the dot.com millionaire crowd of the 1990s, but a new generation of social entrepreneurs, future societal leaders and statesmen who are convinced that something is happening in the world, that it is time for a new energy, a new direction and new way of doing things. In science, art, health—and just about every other arena—there is a momentum building.

But the idealism still has to face a glaring reality: in history there have been many such movements, and most of them have failed. Pure and simple. Failed.

The ones that succeeded, such as the generation of American Founding, the period of Abraham Lincoln, Gandhi's successful revolution and Martin Luther King Jr.'s after him, did so in two waves: a wave of great leaders, preceded by a wave of great teachers. These are the two towers of any successful generation.[1] Without both, no generation effectively achieves its potential. Without one, the other never materializes. This is the seventh lesson I learned on that fateful day: if we don't have the education, we cannot expect to have the leadership. Thankfully, national leaders from all political views joined with international statesmen to condemn the terrorist attacks and re-focus the nation. But what if the crisis had been longer and harder, what if it was just the beginning of a period of world destabilization and challenge, what if the September morning that opened the Twenty-first

Century was just the beginning of a long day with many challenges ahead? What if?

Do we live in a time after the crisis where we can relax, enjoy, and get back to decades of smooth and routine living? Or are we at the beginning of a century or even a decade of turmoil? More to the point, should we be emphasizing the education of accountants, movie directors and secretaries, or using the educational years to train a generation of leaders, entrepreneurs, and statesmen? John Adams is credited with saying that he studied government and law so that his children could study math and science and his grandchildren art and literature. Which generation are we? And more importantly, which are our children? As I looked into the eyes of fifty young people on September 11, 2001, I saw a generation of leaders.

I also saw a haunting drought of schools teaching leadership or training leaders. I had already written the first edition of *A Thomas Jefferson Education* (which carries the subtitle: *Teaching a Generation of Leaders for the Twenty-first Century*), but on that morning it took on new meaning. The question on my mind as I went home exhausted that night was: "Is the education our children are receiving on par with their potential?" It has plagued me ever since. Between that day and this, I have posed this question to tens of thousands of parents, teachers, administrators, legislators and students, and I have seldom received a satisfactory answer. It is time for a change in our educational system.

We Must Do Better

It has been over six years since the first edition of *A Thomas Jefferson Education* was published. Since that time, my wife Rachel and I, as well as a number of dedicated faculty members and scholars at George Wythe College, have spoken in hundreds of venues to tens of thousands of people about the Thomas Jefferson Education (TJEd) model. We have done so on university campuses, private primary and secondary schools, in public elementary and high schools, and at convention centers, country clubs and town halls to professional educators, homeschooling parents, legislators, corporate executives, and interested community members.

We have met many wonderful people and seen thousands of them apply the Thomas Jefferson Education principles in their homes, schools and organizations. We have made literally thousands of new friends, and we have watched them improve their own education and pass on a higher level of excitement for learning to their colleagues and children. In short, we have witnessed a small revolution as many families, schools and companies have made drastic educational changes and seen the quality of their learning significantly increase.

But it is not enough.

"Is the education our children are receiving on par with their potential?" The answer is still a resounding "no." The current educational system must change. This book is a call to that change. As such, it is obviously both audacious and insufficient. But it is a start. Our children deserve the very best education possible, not the most "realistic." They need, and want, the highest quality education that exists, not the most practical. To those who criticize the Thomas Jefferson Education model, I have learned to simply ask, "When you look into the eyes of your children and grandchildren, when you picture their greatness and potential, do you feel that they are getting the education that is up to par with who they were born to become?"

Genius in Our Homes

Greatness isn't the work of a few geniuses, it is the purpose of each of us. It is why we were born. Every person you have ever met is a genius. Every one. Some of us have chosen not to develop it, but it is there. It is in us. All of us. It is in your spouse. It is in each of your children. You live in a world of geniuses. How can we settle for anything less than the best education? How can we tell our children that mediocre education will do, when greatness is available? Like on the morning of 9/11, other calls will come to our generation in the years ahead, announcing new challenges and introducing new opportunities. Our generation, and that of our children, will face its share of crises, just like every generation in the past. When those calls come, will we be ready?

The answer depends on how we educate the next generation.

CHAPTER TWO

Education Today

"All men who have turned out worth anything
have had the chief hand in their own education."

—*Sir Walter Scott*

Almost everyone agrees that modern American education needs to be improved, but almost nobody agrees on what the "fixes" should be or how they should be implemented. The problems are many and diverse: low test scores, illiteracy in the inner city, violence and crime within the school buildings and grounds, racial tension, moral ambiguity, sexual promiscuity, children raising children, parental non-involvement and neglect, oppressive regulation of teachers, competing agendas from administration and even state and federal programs, the large divide between schools in affluent areas and those in poverty, students who lag behind all other industrial nations in math and science, art and music programs cut due to lack of funding, teaching at the bottom of the professional pay scale, the huge cost of building enough schools to serve the rising generation, and the list could go on. Indeed the so-called debate on education is in its fifth decade, with few solutions, if any, in sight.

The truth is that this debate will continue until we realize that it is a fruitless discussion. Education will never be fixed, and in fact it doesn't need to be fixed. Any effort to "fix education" will fail for two reasons. First, education is so many things to so many people: for some, education means job training, for others it means fixing social problems, still others see education as job security or a source of political clout.[2] Americans love education, believe in education and pay big money for education, but few agree on what it is, what it should accomplish, or what methods should be used to achieve it.

Second, the problems of education seem varied and complex; but the complexity is a myth, rooted in a modern misconception about education and educators. Education can't be fixed as long as we believe this basic myth.

The myth is that it is possible for one human being to educate another.

The fact is that the only person who can fix education is the student. The more popular options—increased funding, bigger schools, vouchers, the proliferation of private or charter schools, more homeschooling, a new initiative by a U.S. President, tougher mandates by Congress—will not and cannot fix education. They may improve it, perhaps even significantly, but only to the extent that individual students determine to educate themselves and then follow through.

Teaching, not education, should be our focus,[3] because great teaching inspires students to educate *themselves*. Jacques Barzun made the case for this in the 1960s, but the educational industry moved on without listening.

Great teaching will solve our educational problems—in public, private and home schools, and at the pre-school, primary, secondary, university and even corporate training and professional mentoring levels. Find a great teacher, in any of these settings, and you will find a group of students diligently, enthusiastically and effectively educating themselves.

Teachers teach and students educate. Students are the only true educators. Historically, every other method of education has failed. Education occurs when students get excited about learning and apply themselves; students do this when they experience great teachers.

Two Types of Teachers

There are two types of great teachers which consistently motivate student-driven education: Mentors and Classics. Mentors meet face-to-face with the student, inspiring through the transfer of knowledge, the force of personality, and individual attention. Classics were created by other great teachers to be experienced in books, art, music and other media.

Any system of education which attempts to separate the student from these teachers, classics and mentors, will be less inspiring and therefore less effective—fewer students will choose to seek an education; and those who do will be less likely to follow through.

As the old saying goes, the best education is a student on one end of a log and Mark Hopkins on the other. Students who spend their afternoons across the log from Plato, Jefferson, Milton, Gandhi, Shakespeare and a caring and nurturing parent or other mentor are almost guaranteed a superb education because they will do the necessary hard work. Too often, however, it seems that so-called educators obscure rather than enlighten the views of these great minds, ignore rather than compare, ridicule rather than read.

A generation of students have, like Shakespeare's Ophelia, turned education over to others: "I do not know, my lord, what I should think," and a generation of so-called educators have responded like Polonius: "I'll teach you: think yourself a baby …"[4] In this environment, "teach me" has come to mean "entertain me," "tell me what to think and I'll parrot it back to you," or "hand it to me on a silver platter." But none of these are teaching—or learning.

My Children Deserve Better Than This, But This Is All I Know!

Without great teaching, through mentors and classics, the most that schools can offer is socialization, which they often defend as though it were the primary objective of learning. Some private schools offer a better learning environment than most public schools—but they only help students educate themselves more effectively in direct proportion to their higher rate of great teaching, mentoring and use of the classics. And while some homeschools, charter schools, and voucher-supported schools boast better curricula and higher test scores, again the superiorities are rooted in personalized mentoring. Alternative schools and homes which lack effective teaching, either by a mentor or the classics (or both), tend toward mediocrity or fail altogether. And public, private or college-level teachers who adopt the classics/mentors approach, often against great odds, are likely to inspire students to quality education.

Schools were historically created by parents to allow great teachers—mentors and classics—to inspire students to seek learning and then guide students on their path to a quality education. Then schools were attacked by political agendas from both sides: Conservatives felt that the expense of education should be justified by training students for the job market, and Liberals saw schools as a perfect place to gain support for social agendas ranging from civil rights to environmentalism.

By the mid-2000s, parents must search in vain for schools that *educate*. Few parents realize that the problem is rooted in the very foundation of the system. People cannot be educated unless they *choose to seek education*, and they seek it when they are *inspired by great teachers*, past and present. Parents and students who base their curriculum on job training or social change may end up highly trained or passionately engaged in reform, but they will likely leave school *undereducated*.

Most modern teachers, including those parents who deal with the problem by teaching their children at home, often find that their own educational experience is a real hindrance. How does a generation that grew up uninitiated in the classics now pass on mentoring in classic works to the next generation? We know our children deserve better than what we can offer at home or school, but what can we do?

Finding a Mentor

Years ago, I asked the same question. Having studied with nearly straight "A's" in both high school and a respected private university, I faced a dilemma. I had scholarships, career opportunities, and "great expectations" (though I didn't know what that meant at the time), but I knew something that none of my professors or academic counselors seemed to appreciate: I didn't have an education. I had impressive grades and was on track for a respected diploma and some skills and talents, but I really didn't have an education—and I knew it.

I also knew enough to realize that those who really make a difference in society have a quality education. I also had a new baby son whom I wanted to see get the best out of life. But where to go for an education? About this time, I remembered a speech I had heard at a weekend retreat. I was so inspired that I asked the speaker for some recommended readings, which he supplied. Several years later, when I faced my dilemma (I needed an education and hadn't found it in the schools), I called this speaker and asked for his help. He sent me on a search of the classics. As part of this change, I left a large, respected university to study with a small, unaccredited Bible school. Although I was concerned about the impact on my life, including future credibility and job security, I knew that I had to choose whether to focus on the *quality* and *excellence* my new mentorial education offered or the more typical career training I was getting at the big university. I liked the university, and still consider it a very good school. But I had experienced both types of learning, and I knew in my heart that I had to choose the highest quality education I could find.

Teachers Teach, Students Educate

After several years of mentors and classics, and over a decade of teaching at George Wythe College as a mentor and later mentor of mentors, I have learned that all education boils down to two things: the student putting in the work to educate himself, and the teacher getting the student's attention long enough and deeply enough to get him started and help him keep going.

It is amazing to me how often these basics are missing. At George Wythe College, we actively recruit public, private and homeschoolers, and few freshmen from any of the three have a solid education. Many applicants have good grades, impressive transcripts and high test scores, but when closely scrutinized they are poor writers, poor calculators, and poor readers; consequently, they are poor thinkers. In short, they have learned to play the academic game well, but they are uneducated.

My research and association with other college administrators and teachers assures me that my experience is far from isolated. "Jeffery Hart, an English Professor at Dartmouth, discovered this sad state of affairs for himself while teaching a freshman composition course in 1988. He assigned the class to read Allan Bloom's book *The Closing of the American Mind*. When he asked them what they thought of it, they replied that they hated it. 'Oh yes, they understood perfectly well what Bloom was saying: that they were ignorant, that they believed in cliches, that their education so far had been dangerous piffle and that what they were about to receive was not likely to be any better. No wonder they hated it. After all, they were the best and brightest, Ivy Leaguers with stratospheric SAT scores, the Masters of the Universe.'

"Then Professor Hart launched into an impromptu quiz. 'Could anyone (in the class of 25 students) say anything about the Mayflower Compact? Complete silence. John Locke? Nope. James Madison? Silentia. Magna Carta? The Spanish Armada? The Battle of Yorktown? The Bull Moose party? Don Giovanni? William James? The Tenth Amendment? Zero. Zilch. Forget it. The embarrassment was acute.'"[5]

And from the student perspective: "Karen E. King, a junior International Relations major at American university, expresses well the difficulties that are encountered: 'I came to college to study International Relations within the framework of a well-rounded liberal arts education. I want to understand Western Civilization and how it developed, and be able to speak intelligently on the basic subjects that people have been learning for hundreds of years, things like great literature and history. This, I always assumed, was the definition of being 'educated.' So can someone explain to me why some of America's leading colleges and universities are no longer requiring students to study…history, philosophy, math or science? There has been a purging from the curriculum of many of the required basic survey courses that used to familiarize students with the historical, cultural, political, and scientific foundations of their society….Excuse me, but…I think American colleges and universities are becoming so 'flexible' students can graduate without learning a whole lot."[6]

Problems versus *Difficulties*

What nobody seems willing to say openly anymore, perhaps for fear of turning students away, is that getting an education is *their* job, and that it is a supremely difficult job. Mortimer Adler got it right when he titled an article, "An Invitation to the Pain of Learning." For anyone to get an education, in our modern times or in any times, teachers and students must squarely face what Jacques Barzun called, "the difficulties of schooling, which do not change. Please note: the difficulties, not the problems. Problems are solved or disappear with the revolving times. Difficulties remain. It will always be difficult to teach well, to learn accurately; to read, to write, and count readily and competently; to acquire a sense of history and develop a taste for literature and the arts—in short, to instruct and start one's education or another's."[7] Or as Adler put it: "The kindergarten spirit of playing at education pervades our colleges. Most college students get their first taste of studying as really hard work, requiring mental strain and continual labor, only when they enter law or medical school. Those who do not enter the professions find out what working at anything really means only when they start to earn a living…. But even those who…gradually come to realize the connection between work, pain, and earning…seldom if ever make a similar connection of pain and work with learning. 'Learning' is what they did in college, and they know that that had very little to do with pain and work."[8]

Education for the Twenty-first Century

The solution to the American Education Question is to focus on great teaching rather than education. Each semester at George Wythe College I am moved by a new class of young people who literally come alive during four months of coming face-to-face with greatness in mentors and classics. Suddenly learning is magic, like falling in love; the passion returns and doors and eyes open and students become thinkers, creators, and leaders. The same thing happens wherever the classics/mentors model is applied.

If our schools—public, private and home—return to great teaching, mentors and classics, students will begin doing the hard work of educating themselves and the myriad so-called education problems will be solved.

Parents must lead the charge. Most public and private school teachers—and there are many good ones—are not in a position to change the current environment. Nor are many legislatures or school boards likely to adopt the classics/mentors model. Parents must do it in their own learning, and take their resources to schools and teachers that do it effectively for their children. Homeschool can be an ideal place to do it for parents who will take real leadership, but all types of education will change if parents lead the charge. In fact, if even a significant few do it effectively, public and private schools will have real incentive (spurred by competition) to follow suit. The resultant educational renaissance will empower and reward great teachers, and their children and students will be the only true educators that exist—self-educators

But how should parents proceed?

CHAPTER THREE

Three Systems of Schooling

*"Teaching, like farming and healing, is a cooperative art.
Understanding this, Comenius in* The Great Didactic *again and
again compares the cultivation of the mind with the cultivation of the
field; so, too, Plato compares the teacher's art with the physician's."*

*"…only when teachers realize that the principal cause of learning
that occurs in a student is the activity of the student's own mind
do they assume the role of cooperative artists.
While the activity of the learner's mind is the principal cause
of all learning, it is not the sole cause. Here the teacher
steps in as a secondary and cooperative cause."*

*"Like the farmer and the physician, the teacher must be sensitive to
the natural process that his art should help bring to its fullest frui-
tion—the natural process of learning. It is the nature of human
learning that determines the strategy and tactics of teaching."*

—*Mortimer J. Adler*

O n the first day of school, the little boy waved to his mother
and turned to run down the bright hallway to class. His
teacher smiled and pointed out his desk. "This is going to
be great," he thought. "I love to learn new things." After a few fun
stories, the teacher handed out crayons and paper and announced
that it was time to draw a picture. The little boy enthusiastically

grabbed the crayons and began to imagine all the things he could draw: mountains, lakes, airplanes, his family, his dog, the ocean, the stars at night...

Hundreds of ideas raced through his creative little mind.

His teacher, seeing that he had started drawing, stopped him and said that today the class would be drawing flowers. The boy's mind again ran wild: daisies, daffodils, roses, carnations, violets, lilacs, pansies, mixed bouquets, green gardens full of rainbows of colors...

The teacher again interrupted, informing the class that today they would be drawing a certain kind of flower.

Taking colored chalk, the teacher went to the board and drew a green stem, with two leaves, and four identical pink petals. The little boy, eager to please, dutifully copied her drawing.

After several attempts, his drawing looked exactly like hers. The teacher congratulated him for doing such good work.

As the school year passed, the little boy became a very good student; he learned to listen, obey instructions and get the right answers on tests. His parents were very proud of him, and his teacher was impressed with his excellent progress.

When the next school year arrived, the boy had done so well in his classes that he was enrolled in an accelerated program. During the first week of class, the teacher handed out crayons and paper and announced that it was time to draw a picture. The little boy, still in love with art, enthusiastically picked up his crayons and waited for instructions.

After several minutes the teacher noticed that the little boy wasn't drawing. "Why haven't you started?" she asked. "Don't you like to draw?"

"I love to draw," responded the little boy, "but I was waiting for you to tell us what the assignment is."

"Just draw whatever you want," the teacher smiled and left the little boy to his creativity.

The little boy sat for a long time, watching the minutes tick off the clock and wondering what he should draw. Nothing came to mind.

Finally, in a burst of creative inspiration, he picked up his crayons and began to draw:

A green stem, with two leaves, and four identical pink petals.[9]

The story is indicative of an entire generation of American education, which has been called "the cloning of the American mind." Fortunately, the tragedy is not complete because many parents across the nation are reaffirming their role in educating their children.

The Coming Renaissance in Education

A renaissance is coming to American education, and frankly homeschoolers are uniquely positioned to take advantage of it. All parents can do it, regardless of the geography of their children's learning environment, by emphasizing the highest levels of quality and excellence and settling for nothing less in the education of their children. In history, and today, there are three major types of schooling:

1 *Conveyor Belt education*, which tries to prepare everyone for a job, any job, by teaching them *what* to think. This includes rudimentary skills designed to fit them to function in society. Most public schools are conveyor belt schools, though there are many excellent teachers in the public system who use leadership methods.

2 *Professional education*—from apprenticeship and trade schools to law, medical and MBA programs—which creates specialists by teaching them *when* to think.

3 *Leadership education*, which I call "Thomas Jefferson Education," teaches students *how* to think and prepares them to be leaders in their homes and communities, entrepreneurs in business, and statesmen in government.

Each of the three major educational systems has its own goals, methods and curricula, and each prepares its students for certain types of careers and lifestyles. Educators and parents at all levels benefit from understanding all three systems.

The Conveyor Belt System

Historically the primary goal of public schools, the reason they were instituted, was to educate the poor so they could get a job and take their place in society. The middle class already had private schools and apprenticeships, and the wealthy were tutored at home.

Successful nations in history have had professional schools and leadership education, which complement each other. In class societies, the middle classes have tended toward the professions while the aristocracy received leadership education.[10] Of course, that left out the lower classes, so many nations established public schools to educate the poor. This always improved the nation— delinquency, poverty and enslavement were replaced with widespread literacy and functionality, with resulting increased prosperity and opportunity.

In addition to these considerable benefits of public schools, they often came with a down side. Consider two of the most successful cases: Eighteenth Century Germany, and Nineteenth Century Britain. Each instituted public schools to educate the poor, and the standard of living increased. But eventually the professional and leadership schools deteriorated because they simply couldn't compete with free, government-subsidized schools.

In each case the educational system and later the governmental system collapsed or at least convulsed. The lesson seems to be that if you have all three systems working together, society benefits. But when nearly everyone is getting an education for the poor and hardly anyone is being trained as a leader, the whole nation suffers. Conveyor belts may have an important place in society, but it is essential that they don't become a monopoly and that professional and leadership training schools are maintained.

The Professional System

The second type of education is the professional system. Private schools arose from the apprenticeship tradition of training youth for specific trades or professions. From kindergarten through the twelfth grade, the purpose of prep schools is to get students into college or technical school; then it is to get them into a trade or law school, CPA or MBA program, medical school, etc.

This is done by teaching them *when* to think. The law student is trained to handle legal issues, the medical student to effectively handle a medical situation, the manager a business concern. Such students are trained to be creative, to pull together information and use it to make decisions and marshal the talents and resources under their stewardship. Their specialized knowledge makes them valuable as experts in their field, and an important part of an interdependent system where *other* experts tell them when their knowledge is to be applied and what to do outside the scope of their expertise.

The professional system does what it's designed to do—create expertise. And if you need a doctor, a lawyer or a manager for your business, you are glad they are well prepared. The professional system has been very effective in achieving its goals, but it is not a substitute for leadership training.

The Leadership System

The third educational system is leadership preparation, which has three primary goals. First, its purpose is to train thinkers, leaders, entrepreneurs and statesmen—individuals with the character, competence and capacity to do the right thing and do it *well* in business, government, church, school, family, entertainment, research and other organizations.

The second goal is to perpetuate freedom, to prepare people who know what freedom is, what is required to maintain it, and who exert the will to do what is required. These two goals are accomplished by the third: teaching students *how* to think. Those who know how to think are able to lead effectively and are able to help society remain free and prosperous. Those who know only *what* to think or *when*, no matter how valuable their contributions to society, are not capable of maintaining freedom or leading us to real progress without additional leadership skills. The success and perpetuity of our "American way of life" depend upon leadership education.

Leadership education can be found in certain public school classrooms, a few private and charter schools, and many homeschools. Of course, there are conveyor belt homeschools just as there are leadership public classrooms. Unfortunately, many homeschools are considered inferior by other schools; and the antipathy and relative contempt seem to be mutual in most cases. In truth, there are high quality public schools, private schools and homeschools, just as there are mediocre and poor ones. The key is for parents to find the best education possible for their children and implement it. Parents should choose the school that offers the best educational opportunity for their child.

Despite current stigmas, homeschool is one legitimate option. Homeschooling has a long and successful tradition. Actually, it has two traditions: first, the very wealthy have always educated their children at home, some through professional tutors and others with the parents as mentors; and second, many of the greatest thinkers, leaders, statesmen, entrepreneurs, scientists and artists of history were self-educated.

Wherever the student sits to study, at public or private school, or at home, leadership education is based on several powerful traditions: student-driven learning, great teachers, mentors, classics, and hard work. Together these form the tradition of leadership education, what I call Thomas Jefferson Education, a tradition which is sorely needed in modern America.

I am firmly convinced that Thomas Jefferson Education is the direction education must, and will, take in the coming decades. Abraham Lincoln is credited with saying, "The philosophy of the schoolroom in one generation will be the philosophy of government in the next."[11] This thought has brought me much hope as

I have seen the future in the faces of thousands of parents and teachers I have spoken with across the nation.

I have been so impressed with the parents, public and private school teachers, college and university professors, and a few excellent private and charter schools that are applying the principles of Thomas Jefferson Education. Wherever the elements of Jefferson Education are present, parents and teachers nearly all have in common courage, energy and dedication. The future is in good hands with their children and students at the helm. But all of us need to understand all three systems of education.

Conveyor Belt Methods

Not only are the goals of each system very different, but also the methods. Most public schools use what I call the "Soviet conveyor belt" method. They are set up like a factory: everyone in the class gets the same education at the same age from the same textbooks, and they are tested the same and graded based upon the same scale regardless of their individual interests, talents or goals.

The goal is to give students the same ideas, and to grade and rank them according to their conformity with these ideas. In this system you go down the factory line, first grade, second grade, third grade, with a factory worker at each station, being assembled with certain parts (the curriculum) at a certain point in a certain way from a common book or manual. Of course, all of the products (students) are fitted with the same parts (called "education") as everyone else on the conveyor belt. When you finish twelfth grade, you get a stamp (diploma) on your forehead signifying that you are a finished product ready to be sold to the job market.

The "Soviet" part of it is that standards and grade levels are set at a low enough level that virtually everyone can get through and be a finished product. What happens if you try to get ahead? A factory worker moves you back into place. What if you get behind? A "special" worker pulls you up to speed.

Each of us who has gone through this system can name

notable exceptions to this model—usually great teachers. I'll say a lot more about these quality teachers in a later chapter. For all the good these wonderful educators do in individual lives, the *system* is still a factory which idealizes social and intellectual conformity. If you feel that this system is best for your child, make sure he or she has a great teacher—and stay closely involved with the teacher and even help her understand Thomas Jefferson Education principles.

The Competitive Conveyor Belt

The methodology of the professional system is similar, but it is competitive; the standards are set by the highest 10-15%. In other words, if you want to make it into law school, medical school, the premier MBA programs at the most prestigious Ivy League schools, you have to test in the higher percentiles. But once you're in that percentile, once you make it and say, "I'm at Harvard," you are required to get on the conveyor belt for several years until they stamp another diploma on your forehead. You say, "But I want to think; I want to be a leader." The institutional response is that there is time for that later, after you have graduated; for now you need to focus on your conveyor belt studies.

Of course, this type of focus is mandated in order to really learn the profession. But when and where does the leadership training come? Where are the schools which offer it?

The Leadership Crisis

These same three systems have existed for a long time, and free and prosperous nations have always had a strong leader education system. When I teach this, people often say at this point, "Well, in our society we just go to public school. That's how everybody does it, that's how the system has worked for a long time." In fact, our modern system is a fairly recent development. Only in the last seventy years has it become the predominant system. In the history of education, the current American system is very non-traditional, very different from what has been done for generations. Almost everybody in America today is getting the kind of education that has historically been reserved for those who simply had no other options. Where this used to include the poor and lower classes, today it has become almost universal.

What happens when a society does not prepare leaders? We get managers and professionals leading in areas they have no training for, such as government, and we get a nation of followers who see no problem with that because they have no experience with anything else. In a nation where the government is supposed to be the servant of the people, it is easy to see that our traditional form of government and its cultural underpinnings will deteriorate beyond repair if the citizen neglects to fit himself for leadership; eventually the result is widespread specialization complemented by arrogance, pride and general ignorance. This was the legacy of Germany in the 1930s—a highly trained but uneducated people easily swayed by Hitler.

In the past, the traditional leadership pool—the wealthy and the aristocracy—have always been educated with mentors and tutors, and then at prep schools which use the classics/mentors approach. There's a reason for that: the mentor system creates statesmen. Without such a system, you just don't get the same caliber of leaders. And when a few do emerge, you will almost certainly find that they have a leader education background. Of course, in America we don't have an aristocracy and don't want one, so leaders must come from all classes—what Jefferson called the "natural aristocracy."[12] But if they are to be entrepreneurs and statesmen, they must be trained as entrepreneurs and statesmen by the curriculum and methods used to train leaders throughout history.

"What About Their Social Life?"

The actual curriculum of the public school system is about 75% social and 25% skills. When I present this to public school teachers, many of them raise their hands and say something like, "75%

is low on that. It's at least 85% and probably more." The real goals of public school are social more than academic.[13] If you doubt it, pull your kids out of school to start homeschooling, and see what your friends and family say. I'll bet you won't be asked, "Hey, what about their academics?" But I guarantee you someone will ask, "What about their *social* life?"

Don't just ignore the question, it is a valid one. We live in society and most of us choose to interact with others. But the real question should be, "What are you socializing them *for*?" Everybody is socialized in one way or another. Children aren't going to grow up and never spend time with other people. What people usually mean is, "Will they seem normal and well-adjusted, or backward and strange?" In most cases that depends on the parents. If parents are so-called "backward and strange," chances are their kids will be also—even if they are in public school. In fact, such children will likely be less "normal" when they reach early adulthood, given the teasing and rejection they are almost sure to feel in school. At least in homeschool, their confidence is supported and they have a strong chance of getting a good education without their love of learning being destroyed by an artificial social and class structure which dominates the hallways, locker rooms and classrooms. Many of those who tend to struggle socially anyway may be better off in a homeschool than on the conveyor belt.

If your children are educated at school, you still need to give thought to their socialization. Are they perhaps being socialized in bad ways? Are there opportunities or lessons you can give them that will improve their socialization? All parents should consider socialization an important part of growing up.

But consider the question at a deeper level. The highest level of socialization, the ideal, means the ability to effectively work with people of all backgrounds, stations, and positions, of really caring about them and being able to build and maintain long term, nurturing relationships. The conveyor belt, by its very nature, discourages this. Spending your time with the older sixth graders or the cheerleaders or whatever group is seen as most popular often earns you the title of snob, unless you are "one of them." And if you are a member of the "in" group, socializing with those "below" your station is frowned upon and discouraged—except by parents and teachers, who are very impressed with you, earning you a reputation as "teacher's pet." Much of this is carried into college and career and even into politics and pettiness in the work place.

It is not a great stretch of the imagination to see how the grouping of children according to birth year can breed envy of those older, contempt for those younger, and alienation from siblings. Spending all day in an institution run by adults (each equally requiring and supposedly deserving of respect and unfailing obedience) can provide competition in a child's mind and heart for loyalty to and trust in his parents and the family's own culture and values. The fact that most of our nation's children are "socialized" in this system defines popular culture on those terms. Parents must be alert and active to combat these pressures, even if the children are schooled at home, and especially if they attend public or private school. The survival of our families and the souls of our children depends upon it.

As one national commentator mused: "Over the past two years, Lorena has become interested in teaching our daughter ourselves, and she's investigated all the data about reading ability and math scores. But a single fact has brought me around to think she's right about homeschooling Faith. In the midst of America's endless argument about charter schools and vouchers, parental choice and teacher's unions, I hear almost no one asserting that one of the things education should aim at is to produce children who have what Aristotle called a great soul.

"I can't pretend my wife and I have much idea about how to go about that. But homeschooling still seems worth trying, if only because we haven't discovered many professional teachers who have much idea either—or many who believe even in the possibility of great souls anymore."[14]

In fairness, there are many examples of struggling youngsters being taken under the wing of a caring teacher, principal or coach and really excelling—academically and socially. But this can as easily be a parent as a teacher. Public schools also have numerous socializing failures. The fact is, both homeschools and public schools have socializing successes and failures. Most of us know individual examples of both. But you can't legitimately criticize homeschooling for not socializing, when its successes compete favorably with public and private schools. For the most part homeschool avoids the negative social pressures of gangs, drugs, cliques, etc.

As a parent, instead of finding ways to defend against this frustrating question ("What about their social?"), give some real thought to how you can help your students be as highly prepared as possible with social skills as well as scholarship. The royalty and super-rich, and in recent decades the entertainment industry—establishers of social norms—have done academics at home through mentors and socialized their children in non-school events. Homeschool is natural to socializing future leaders who don't feel compelled to follow the crowd or bend to social pressure, but who do feel at ease with others and work well in society.

This takes some planning and work; it probably won't just happen. You must model it for them, even if it means getting out of your comfort zone, and give them opportunities to be where they can experience for themselves. If you get them involved in such settings starting when they are young, they will be socialized like leaders always have been—by interacting with adults and others of all ages from their early years, and being much more comfortable in adult work, social and other settings than their contemporaries.

Social interaction with peers is also a homeschool natural. Brian Ray of the National Home Education Research Institute found the following: The typical homeschooled child is regularly involved in 5.2 on-going social activities outside the home, including dance classes, music lessons, little league sports, scout troops, church groups, and neighborhood play; while average test scores for homeschooled children are 30 to 37 percentile points higher than those of public school students.[15]

In summary, don't just ignore the most asked question about homeschooling. Homeschool is uniquely designed to be a wonderful place to socialize children and youth—with their peers and in interaction with adults. With a little planning, the right kind of socialization can be one of the real strengths of homeschool; it certainly has been for the royalty and wealthy through history.

Again, and this bears repeating, if you are using another quality setting to educate your children, say a charter or private school, or even a public school, be sure to pay attention to their socialization. Conveyor belt socialization will likely have negative aspects that you will need to mitigate, and without other considered influences being added to the mix, such socialization will not prepare them for leadership.

The Key to Leadership Education

The fundamental difference between leadership education and the other types of learning, is that the leadership curriculum is *individualized*. Find a great leader in history, and you will find an individualized education. The place to begin individualization is in understanding the developmental process that underpins great education. We call this the Phases of Learning. These Phases were first noted and identified in our research of the education of Thomas Jefferson, and were later seen to be a pattern of many luminaries in history who lived exemplary lives and changed the world for good. These phases have been defined and discussed exhaustively, both from a philosophical and an applicational standpoint, in our book on the Phases of Learning; however, a brief summary as a foundation for further discussion of TJEd is in order here.

Core Phase

At the center of each individual's personality and development is the Core Phase. The establishment of the Core occurs roughly between the years of 0-8; the maintenance and nourishment of the Core is a life-long process. During Core Phase, critical lessons of life are learned and assumptions are made that define the individual's concept of self, family, and the beginnings of their broader worldview. During this phase attention should be given above all to the nurture of a happy, interactive, confident child through the lessons that occur naturally during work and play in the family setting. Any programming of learning which does not fit this description can imperil the critical lessons to be learned in this phase. Such lessons are often extremely difficult to assimilate as effectively later.

Home is the ideal venue for the Core Phase, and "homeschool" in the Core is a product of the structure and flow of family life. This consists of the lessons of good/bad, right/wrong, true/false, and is accomplished through work/play. The acquisition of "scholarly" skills is not as important as these lessons during this phase. Ample research supports the position that later readers are life-long readers, and that much harm is done to the child who feels pressured to excel, is labeled as "slow," or in any way is made to feel "unacceptable" during this phase, especially in relation to academic performance. A child who plays at and practices learning throughout the Core Phase will approach skills acquisition at the self-appropriate time and pace with relish and self-confidence as her aptitude increases and the meaning of the tasks gains context through her experiences. The biggest need during this phase—for all children, wherever they are schooled—is the rich learning environment and family culture of self-education that are inherent in the TJEd model home. For children who are schooled away from home, this phase is if anything more important than for homeschoolers.

Love of Learning Phase

Following a successful Core Phase, a child will naturally transition to what we call "Love of Learning." During this period, a child will commonly play at projects and skills which builds his repertoire of understanding and prowess. During Love of Learning, which typically runs more or less between the ages of 8-12 (often earlier for girls than for boys), the time in the day devoted to learning will gradually increase over time to a number of hours a day by the time the student transitions to Scholar Phase.

In Love of Learning Phase, the child builds upon the foundation of the Core Phase and continues on to form his assumptions of identity and community. The Love of Learner is ripe for exposure to the many areas of human knowledge, with a focus on that which he can experience on his level. Some children may have particular gifts or aptitude in a more technical area with established norms, and insofar as their involvement is exploratory and interest driven, it is to be encouraged. In contrast, special care should still be given for a time to allow for personal expression without negative feedback.

By this we do not mean that there is no discipline in the home. In the areas of family routine and the individual's obligations to follow house rules and contribute to the running of the home and family, rules and consequences are essential to the child's sense of security and accomplishment. Rather, in the areas of exploration and skills building, the parent/mentor should be wary of establishing premature and unnecessary standards of "correctness" on points that will later be obvious and require no criticism.

For example, the requirement to subject a daily journal to proofreading can stifle a love of self-expression. To make an issue of numbers printed backward during Love of Learning can leave a child feeling defensive toward the very person she should ideally look to for help when she has a desire to "do it right" or wants to make a good impression with others who may view her work.

As noted previously, Thomas Jefferson Education has high standards of quality. These are learned in the early years through family work and routine rather than in perfectionism in academic skills. Later, in Scholar and Depth Phases, the temperament and aptitude of the student not only allow for serious critique and review, they require it.

The TJEd home will facilitate a successful Love of Learning Phase as parents and older siblings model the behaviors of study, self-discipline, passion for learning, a sense of personal mission and a habit of service in and out of the home.

Scholar Phase

Scholar Phase (often, but not always, from ages 12-16) typically ensues with the onset of puberty and is marked by a change in the student's physical, emotional and social expression. With these changes come a readiness to apply a new level of effort to personal and academic achievement through a process of commitments and accountability. The young Scholar should have additional privileges (exempted from some chores such as "errand running," diaper changing, dishes, or whatever seems appropriate in the individual situation) as a young adult—rather than a teenager. He should also have defined responsibilities (as opposed to just tasks and jobs). For example, a Scholar Contract may define some certain 25-50 hours per week when the parents facilitate uninterrupted study time, while at the same time the Scholar has a list of agreed upon responsibilities (e.g. all of the laundry, or dinner every night, or all yard maintenance, or some other full-charge situation) which is clearly and simply defined.

The Scholar should ideally be exposed to a variety of options in materials and classic works, and be encouraged both morally and substantively to gain experience and exposure to great ideas—through book discussions, peer-group classes, or other enticing experiences that feed the need for social as well as intellectual stimulation.

Scholar Phase is a time to study "everything under the sun," to read, study science and math, practice art and study the great artists, and cover every topic and subject in a spirit of passion and excitement for learning. It is a time to study long hours, to work hard at learning because you love it, and to ponder, think, read, write, listen, discuss, debate, analyze and learn. It is the time to lose your life in study—and if it doesn't happen in youth, it is very difficult to recreate later.

Depth Phase

Depth Phase (ideally between 16-22) is characterized by a profound hunger to prepare for oncoming responsibilities and future contributions in society. This hunger leads a Scholar to acknowledge his or her limitations, and the limitations of the current mentorial arrangement, and to submit to the grueling expectations of a mentor at a new and higher level. For most, this is best accomplished in a college setting.

The moral support of others similarly engaged, the networking with those who are also mission-oriented, the challenge of having your grand ideas revealed to be limited or ineffectual, the opportunity for exposure to peers with new and thought-provoking solutions to age-old problems, and the interaction with mentors with an obsession for excellence and the character and competence to demand it, is the ideal culmination for the years of earlier training in the leadership model. This college experience simply must be individualized. Of course, that means that somebody must do the individualizing. Great education means self-education, but at some point it must also mean having a great mentor. In the history of the world, the combination of classics and mentors has been the method of obtaining all of the necessary knowledge, traits and skills. Classics and mentors are the foundation of leadership education, which is the best preparation for professional training, leadership roles, and for life itself. The success of leadership education ultimately hinges on one thing—the mentor.

CHAPTER FOUR

Mentoring

*"For learning requires a mentor—an Athena, a Virgil, a Beatrice—
to lead and teach, guide and instruct...showing their charges
how to learn, stepping back when the pupil begins to
see and to understand on his own."*

—L. Cowan

*"Since learning...is essentially a process of discovery, the teacher's
art consists largely in devices whereby one individual can help
another to lift himself up from a state of knowing and understanding
less to knowing and understanding more. Left to his own devices,
the learner would not get very far unless he asked himself questions,
perceived problems to be solved, suffered puzzlement over dilemmas,
put himself under the necessity of following out the implications
of this hypothesis or that, made observations and weighted
the evidence for alternative hypotheses . . ."*

—Mortimer J. Adler

A s stated previously, find a great leader in history, and
you will nearly always find two central elements of their
education—classics and mentors. From Lincoln, Jefferson
and Washington to Gandhi, Newton and John Locke, to Abigail
Adams, Mother Theresa and Joan of Arc—great men and women
of history studied other great men and women. Whatever the

culture, look at its greatest leaders and you will almost always find that they were guided by at least one outstanding mentor and made a lifetime study of classic works.

Thomas Jefferson is a model of this system. He was one of the best students in history, and his education is in many ways a model for successful leadership education today. "Thomas Jefferson Education" is too often missing in modern educational institutions. The basic tenets of Thomas Jefferson Education are classics and mentors, depth and breadth, quality and application.

Depth and breadth mean really paying the price to get a great education, a superb knowledge base. Jefferson set the tone for this. In addition to his articulate mastery of English that led his peers to tap him for the job of drafting the *Declaration of Independence*, Jefferson learned to speak Latin, Greek, Spanish, Italian, French and more than ten Native American dialects. His mastery went beyond the modern equivalent of college degrees in law, physics, mathematics, theology, philosophy, zoology, and chemistry.

He was a plantation owner, accomplished attorney, businessman and inventor. He served as United States Minister to France, Secretary of State, Vice President and President of the United States. He was the founder, president, and director of one of America's first universities. He wrote not only the *Declaration of Independence*, but also the *Statute for Religious Freedom*, and many other notable works. His education was such that President John F. Kennedy, at a White House dinner honoring a host of Nobel Prize winners, described the guests as: "The most extraordinary collection of talent and human knowledge that has ever been gathered together at the White House—with the possible exception of when Thomas Jefferson dined alone."[16]

Jefferson learned from his mentors that only quality work was acceptable and that this often meant doing things over and over. Application of knowledge to the real world is essential; no education is complete, or even particularly valuable, unless the student uses what he or she has learned to serve the community, family, society and God.

To summarize, effective education in the tradition of Thomas Jefferson requires depth and breadth of knowledge, quality work on the part of each student, and real world application of that knowledge in a way that helps others. The two keys to obtaining these are classics and mentors.

The George Wythe Method

A good mentor is someone of high moral character who is more advanced than the student and can guide his or her learning. Parents are the natural mentors of children. They can be very effective in getting the student started on a lifetime plan for success, especially if they use some of the key techniques perfected by the great mentors of history. Teachers, professors, coaches, music instructors, employers, neighbors and community leaders can also be good mentors.

My favorite model of how to mentor is George Wythe, the mentor of Thomas Jefferson. George Wythe was a signer of the *Declaration of Independence* and a delegate to the Constitutional Convention. He was the first law professor in America, a famous judge, and Chancellor of the State of Virginia. Perhaps his most lasting contribution was as mentor to two future U.S. Presidents, two Supreme Court Justices, and a number of future senators, representatives, governors and judges. Let's consider how the methods he used can be applied in our modern schools—public, private and home—in order to train leaders for the future.

A number of years ago I helped found George Wythe College, and one of my first responsibilities was researching just how Wythe mentored Jefferson. From that intensive research, and years of additional reading and studying, I found Seven Keys of Great Teaching which form the core of great mentoring.

1. Classics, Not Textbooks

Thomas Jefferson's studies with George Wythe were four "years of virtually uninterrupted reading, not only in the law but also in the ancient classics, English literature and general political philosophy. It wasn't so much an apprenticeship for law as it was an apprenticeship for greatness."[17] Allan Bloom said in *The Closing of the American Mind*: "When a youngster like Lincoln sought to educate himself, the immediately obvious things for him to learn were the Bible, Shakespeare and Euclid. Was he really worse off than those who try to find their way through the technical smorgasbord of the current school system, with its utter inability to distinguish between important and unimportant?...I do not believe that my generation, my cousins who have been educated in the American way, all of whom are M.D.s or Ph.D.s, have any comparable learning."[18]

As students become familiar with and eventually conversant with the great ideas of humanity, they learn how to think, how to lead, and how to become great. The classics, by introducing the young mind to the greatest achievements of mankind and the spiritual teachings of inspired individuals, prepare children to become successful human beings, parents and leaders in their own time. As one of my former students and current friends, Tiffany Rhoades Earl, wrote to me in a letter: "I felt my nature change as I read *Les Miserables*. So many unfair circumstances and events happened to Jean Valjean, and he made bad choices. But then he was set free, he had a choice to make, just like all of us do. I found myself hoping that he would finally relinquish his hatred, his hardened heart, and become who he was meant to be. And all of the sudden I found myself yearning to relinquish *my* hatred, *my* hardened heart, to become who I was meant to be. When the Bishop gave him the silver, I found myself somehow changed—forever. This is what a classic does. It changes us. It changed *me*."

Classics also ensure the future of freedom, as Lord Brougham said: "Education makes a people easy to lead, but difficult to drive; easy to govern, but impossible to enslave." He was clearly talking about true liberal arts education, not conveyor belt job training.

2. Mentors, Not Professors

George Wythe built his Depth Phase students' learning around the classics, but each student had a personalized study program designed to fit his individual goals. Someone who approaches twenty students with identical curriculum, methodology, goals and plans is not acting as a mentor. The mentor helps each student identify where he or she is, and then says, "Okay, let's develop a program for you. What do you want to become? What do you want to create? What do you want to learn?" Once the mentor gets the answer from the student, he helps the student develop a personal plan to achieve it. You can't train leaders on a conveyor belt; if you want to teach students *how* to think, their studies must be personalized.

Consider the American Founding generation. From ages 5-12, they were typically taught at home or in local community schools directed by the parents. Some started earlier, others later, according to their interests and talents and direction from their parents. Of course, parents really started teaching them from birth, but somewhere in their early years they began reading classics and discussing them with their mentors. Their curriculum was the Three R's—reading, writing and 'rithmetic—all based upon morality and the classics. They even got their arithmetic from the classics, and the Bible was the core of their learning.

Around ages 13-17, most of the Founding generation went to boarding school and/or college where they took on the classics and went further in depth. Then from 18-21, students went to work or on to professional training. The key point here is that in all these studies, learning was individualized: first by parents at home, then by other mentors at school and college. If they went into law or medicine or a trade, they worked with yet another set of mentors who assessed their strengths and weaknesses and set out to help them achieve success. The system was successful enough that the typical 1789 New York farmer could read and understand the *Federalist Papers*, something many Ph.D. and J.D. students would struggle with today.

The conveyor belt education system has made us more highly trained as a generation, but less educated. Leadership, therefore, is lacking. None of George Wythe's students had quite the same curriculum; each student had a personalized program designed to fit his needs and interests. Our schools—public, private and home—can do the same by simply taking each student as an individual. The classics make individualizing the content simple because the same book can be different for each reading.

3. Inspire, Not Require[19]

If the purpose is to train leaders, it's important not to force the young person through their learning experiences. Force in learning kills the spirit, dampens the passion and destroys the zest and life of learning. Force trains followers, not leaders.

Unfortunately, most of us were conditioned to believe that if we aren't forced to learn, especially something like math or advanced science, we won't do it. In truth, force does teach lessons, but they are the wrong lessons. The negative lessons of force include:

- Do the bare minimum.
- Learning means pleasing the authority figure.
- Learning, schooling and studying are no fun.
- Playing is when you don't have to learn.
- To be a good student I have to study somebody else's interests.
- My own interests must be pursued on my own time, and they aren't as valuable as the "accepted" topics of study.
- If nobody is making me study, I'd rather be entertained than learn.

The list could go on, but the point is that force is a bad method of incentivizing or encouraging learning. Wise parents and teachers learn to inspire their students to intensive self-study, instead of requiring them to follow a pre-formulated curriculum. Just as the Core must be maintained throughout a lifetime, so must the Love of Learning be cultivated through persistent exposure to inspirational and transformational mentors and classics.

Frankly, this is the most challenging part of the Thomas Jefferson Education system—at least for anybody who spent most of their education on the conveyor belt. The truth is that most parents and teachers really prefer force, really like the ability to just assign and demand and mete out consequences. We have been conditioned to believe that this is what education is, that anything else must be less valuable or less effective.

But compare the list of lessons above to the following list of lessons learned by the person who is inspired to get a great education:

- There is so much to learn and it is so exciting.
- Learning is more fun than almost anything.
- I can learn on my own, in a group, or with help from a teacher or parent.
- All I need is a book and I can learn.
- In fact, I can learn even without a book.
- I love learning!
- I am passionately interested in (fill in the blank here, from horses to surfing to dolls to Nancy Drew mysteries, etc.).
- If I do more than is assigned, I'll learn more and have more fun. The assignments are just minimums.
- My thoughts and ideas are as valuable as anybody else's.

Again, the list could go on, but clearly the natural lessons of freely choosing your own education are very valuable. Indeed, freedom is the natural teacher of leadership, just as leadership is the perpetuator of freedom.

The challenge is that most people (with our conveyor belt past) hear the phrase "inspire, not require," and actually translate it more as "*ignore*, not require." Nothing could be further from the truth. Ignoring a child's education won't help him at all, but requiring most of his education is just as damaging. And of the three (ignoring, requiring, and inspiring), the one that demands the most of the teacher, mentor or parent is to inspire.

Inspiring, in contrast to ignoring and forcing, means finding out what the students need and then creatively encouraging them to engage it on their own—with excitement and interest. At least three things are needed to effectively inspire a student to study. First, the student needs to see someone setting the example. Sometimes, this is almost all that is needed. Wherever you find a great teacher who is passionately pursing a great education and positively inviting the students to participate, you'll find a high percentage of inspired students who study hard and learn.

Second, the student needs to understand her options. As a mentor, sit down with the student and tell her the various paths available to her in life. Discuss the consequences of not getting a quality education and the possible results of really applying herself to her studies. Such discussions should not be limited to material results, but also include the joy and excitement of learning. A passion for education is contagious and a teacher who shares will naturally interest those around him.

Third, give the student the choice. Students who are forced to do something will usually resent it, and they won't ever work as hard or supply the same quality of effort as when they freely choose to engage it on their own. If they choose not to study hard, even after you've set a great example and also talked to them about how important and how fun it is, then chances are your forced requirements would have fallen on deaf ears anyway. The level of work and excellence they'll achieve when they do freely pursue something is worth not always feeling the need to push, push, push.

As we've taught seminars on Thomas Jefferson Education across North America, we've run into quite a few teachers who consider themselves "very strict," and also many mothers who admit that they are "Sergeant Mom" and dads who are always giving orders and using force to lead. In nearly all cases, their students identify more with the first list above than the second.

Why not give freedom a try? It actually works. I knew this from my instincts and my research when I wrote the first edition of this book, but we now have literally thousands of parents and students who have personified this principle and achieved incredible results. In the force model of "Require," it is typical to find 14-year-olds who resist more than minimal study each day; but in Thomas Jefferson Education classrooms and homes, it is the norm to have 14-year-olds who study 10 hour days and beg for more. Combined with the other Keys of Great Teaching, that means they get a truly superb education.

4. Structure Time, Not Content

No method of learning is effective without adequate time. Time takes structure. "Structure" is a dangerous word in modern education because most parents and teachers were themselves public schooled. So when, say, a homeschooling parent decides to homeschool, she sets it up the only way she knows how—like a public school. The parents leave the public system for some reason—academic, social, religious, whatever—and try to set up a little public school at home, a little conveyor belt. They decide, "At 8:00 o'clock we're going to do math, and at 8:50 we'll do English, and at 9:40 history," etc. But they can never hope to teach students "what to think" as well as the public conveyor belt with its hallways, lockers, credits, grade levels and bells. If their goal is teaching them how to think, they need to do it the leadership way.

We need structure in order to give adequate time and attention to learning, but the key is to structure the time, not the content. Let me repeat: Structure time, not content. For example, if you set aside five hours a day, five days a week most of the year, with occasional interruptions for activities or trips, and consistently do school during this period, most students will have time to obtain a quality education. For younger children it will be less, and for advanced students it will likely be more. The structure and intensity of the academic schedule progresses from relatively non-existent at the very earliest ages to the almost constant rigors of adolescent and adult scholarship.

More detailed structure may be helpful for a few Scholars who choose to organize *themselves*—as long as you keep it simple, such as: math for at least one hour first thing, essay writing and discussion with the mentor the last hour, and free study in between. Different things work for different students. Remember that the purpose of the structure is simply to ensure that the students have sufficient time to study. The mentor doesn't have to be there the whole time, but should interact often, and the students should be given great freedom to read and study and experiment according to their own interests. Always remember the Phases; this type of structure is usually detrimental before the young student is truly ready for intense study.

5. Quality, Not Conformity

When Scholars do an assignment, either say "great work" or "do it again." You can help them, but have them do most of the work and never accept a low quality submission or performance. Wythe was very demanding this way with Jefferson. Note that we're talking here about more mature students, usually at least 12 and older, not of toddlers and children.

Parents often worry that they aren't really experts, so they hesitate to enforce high standards. And teachers sometimes feel too busy to give assignments *repeat* personal attention. For young children, the Core and Love of Learning are more important than the conformity or quality of work.[20] But at some point in their development you will do them a huge favor if you set up a system of standards *together* and then abide by it. The key is coaching. Think about it. The places where the conveyor belt system gets professional level quality are where they have coaching—athletics, drama, debate, music, etc. This is mentoring, and it is personalized. Students, say the quarterback or the trombone player, are expected to work on it over and over until they get it right. Do the same in academics, and you will eventually get world-class scholarship.

Student papers, reports and assignments must be high quality. For homeschoolers, don't give them grades. Just "great work" or "do it again." For teachers in a public or private school, the "do it again" grade should be used a lot more throughout each term. If they don't like the book or the thing they are studying, discuss it anyway. If their report is vague and they seem bored, ask why. Talk it out, even if their response is negative. For example:

"Well, I just didn't like it because . . ." Whatever their reasons, they are thinking now. Keep questioning them.

What if they say, "I don't want to discuss this book. I hated this book."

"Why did you hate it? What was wrong with it? What was the problem?" Some of the most powerful discussions I've had with students at George Wythe College are about the book *The Lord of the Flies,* because everyone hates it. I hate it myself. My junior English teacher in high school, Mrs. Herrick, asked me about it and my response was, "I hate it." I've never changed my mind about it, though I've reread it a number of times. But she knew to keep talking about it. It's a really good book to hate. But there are some powerful discussions that take place when you say, "Why do you hate it?"

"Because it leaves God out of everything."

"Okay, that's a good reason. Does society ever make that same mistake?"

"That's why I hated it, because our society is getting to be just like that."

"Well, if you were on that island in *The Lord of the Flies,* how would you change things? What would *you* do?"

"I would . . ."

Whatever their answer, you can respond: "Okay, then how are you going to do those same things in our society?"

This is powerful. Take the greatest ideas of humanity and apply them to self and society. Question, probe, ponder, think, discuss, write, apply. Push yourself as a mentor, so that you can push your students. This is the great key to mentoring—lead out by pushing yourself even harder than you push them. And push them by requiring quality work, just like Wythe did with Jefferson.

Educating Leaders

This is how the great leaders of history learned. They read classics and had these sorts of discussions and were really pushed (by inspiration and internal drive, not forced requirements) by mentors; and then when they were in situations where they had to make difficult decisions, the future Lincolns of the world were able to say things like: "No! This is unacceptable. Jane Eyre would have done this, Cicero would have done this, and this is what I'm going to do." If leaders have pondered the great ideas, the great stories, under the guidance of a good mentor, they know what is, and how to choose, the right. The classics become part of their makeup, part of who they are. Their friends and close associates are able to say, "Here's what you should do. Think of Pip. You're making a decision out of pride; it's not going to turn out well." They can back up and say, "You know, you're right."

There's a powerful scene in the Star Trek movie *First Contact* where Captain Picard is about to make a fatal mistake, and another character says something like, "Okay, Ahab, you go right ahead." That changes the whole paradigm for him. "Ahab." He realizes, "I am Ahab," and he starts quoting Melville, and changes his mind. The stories we associate ourselves with, whether of Moses or Hamlet or *Anne of Green Gables*, become powerful in our lives; and when the time comes to make tough decisions, we fall back on them in order to decide. When a person has come face-to-face with George Washington as a central part of her education, or with Esther or Ruth, she stands up in a crisis situation and says, "I will not; neither will you." The classics are a part of her. That's greatness and leadership, and all it takes are classics, mentors and hard work.

6. Simplicity, Not Complexity

To achieve truly excellent education, keep it simple: Read, Write, do Projects and Discuss. The more complex our national curriculum has become, the less educated our society. And it's not just in the United States. You find it in ancient Rome, Greece, Chinese history, Japanese history, many modern nations, and elsewhere. Jefferson didn't have access to our modern "advanced" textbooks and yearly updated curriculum modules or standardized tests. He read the classics, wrote about them, and discussed what he learned with his mentors. George Wythe structured Jefferson's curriculum around these simple items: classics, discussion, projects, writing. Nearly the whole Founding generation did the same, and the further we have moved from this simple formula, the worse our education has become.

What we need to improve education is not more curriculum, but better *education*, and that comes from classics and mentors. With young children you do two things: read them the classics—things at their level like *Black Beauty*, *Charlotte's Web*, the *Little House on the Prairie* series, fables and rhymes—then talk about it with them, teach them lessons. You may want to preview the books beforehand, read them yourself and decide if they are classics. Do they teach the great moral lessons that you want to discuss with your children? If so, read them to the children. Read poems, stories, and brief biographical accounts of great scientists, doctors, mathematicians, artists, statesmen, etc. Most importantly, read them your family history and central religious texts—whatever your faith.

As the children get older, whether they go to school or learn at home, expose them to other things. Increase the depth and the difficulty level, but focus on reading classics and discussing. Of course, you can only mentor them well if *you* read the books too. Read the classic they're reading. If you've read it before, then you have a chance of learning a lot more from it each time through. The more you read it, the more you'll learn. If you read it with your first three children, read it again with the fourth. Or if you teach in a public or private school, read it with each new class. If it isn't worth reading four times, it shouldn't be on your classic list. The fourth child or eighth class will get the better education because you're a better mentor, and each time you read it you'll get something new that you never thought of before. Those new "aha's" are what keep you animated and interesting as a mentor. After you share this new discovery with your fourth child, call the other three and tell them about it. You'll create a lifelong tradition of mentoring and learning that will be passed on to future generations.

Effective Discussions

The key to quality discussion is to have lots of discussions, both planned and spontaneous, about classic and other quality readings. For example, say you and your students are reading Dickens' *Great Expectations*. Pip is the main character. He's a young child, he's poor, no one thinks he'll amount to much in life. Then all of a sudden he gets an anonymous donation of money, so they say, "Pip, you have great expectations, you'll be wonderful." He matures and grows up and has to make some decisions about what's right and wrong and good and bad. He ends up making decisions which lead him in the wrong direction, decisions based on pride. He feels that what is socially acceptable is more important than what he knows is right. He alienates his old friends and the people who supported him because he wants to look right in high society. He makes mistakes and has to deal with the consequences.

These are powerful themes for discussion with your students: how they choose their friends and how they act around them, what is really important in life, what integrity and loyalty are and how they are manifest in our actions, etc. Such subjects can also be powerful catalysts for classroom discussion.

You can do this spontaneously as you are reading and think of something. Or you can set a time to be finished and have a discussion. Better still, have several students and parents read it and come together for a group discussion. You can refer back to the book later on in life when your child is dumping old friends to look good to a more popular crowd. "You have great expectations. Are you sure about this?"

In your discussions, let the students think. Don't just tell them what it said. Ask questions. Suppose one of your students says, "I don't think Pip made a wrong decision, I think he was right." Don't tell him he's wrong. Instead try: "That's really interesting. Would you tell us why?" With Dad and Mom there, and perhaps other children, or in a classroom, this can be a powerful teaching moment.

Writing as Learning

In addition to discussion, encourage them to write about what they are learning as frequently as possible. Then evaluate their writing and give them feedback, which leads to more discussion. They can also give reports to a bigger group or send their papers to others for feedback. Letters to another student about books they both read can be very valuable.

George Wythe had Thomas Jefferson, and his other students, keep what they called a Commonplace Book, which was a journal of what they studied and learned each day. Students could write at least one essay each day, summarizing the main ideas or some new concept they have learned. Mentors look over the essays, and this can lead to more discussion and ideas. In fact, I highly recommend that mentors write a daily essay also, even if it is just a few paragraphs. This is a great way to document your process and progress. It increases daily retention, interest and discussion. It is also very helpful to come back to your notes later and compare them with new facts and ideas you are learning.

This paragraph or essay a day is key to the learning process, and can be used with students at any age and in any topic. With younger children, you may need to write it for them. Ask, "Would you like me to record something for you today?" Then write down the answer. Soon they will be asking you to help them make out the letters and write it down. This will create a habit of recording what is learned and storing it for future use. It will also teach them to write.

At the appropriate time their essays get more advanced; almost without fail they will approach *you* for help in learning the common standards for grammar, spelling and other details, and have them rewrite and polish. Be positive and use restraint. Do not allow yourself to be overanxious to point out the errors of the younger student. You are simply a resource at their disposal, not a critic. Be sure that they are progressing in content and expression first of all. Then, as they are older and you have a formal understanding of your mentorial relationship and of standards of excellence, you can be as demanding as need be to really help them achieve their objectives.

Again, the focus should be on content rather than technique; help them become good and later excellent writers by challenging assumptions, helping them phrase things more accurately and eloquently, and finding ways to use what they have written in real life projects. For example, one of my students at George Wythe College decided to make all of her papers for an advanced Political Science class into something that would have real life impact. She wrote letters to her Congressmen and Governor summarizing the key principles of good government she was learning from the classics and applying them to current issues and challenges. The response was warm at first, and then turned into a dialogue, and ended up with actual legislation and implementation of some of her suggestions. Writing is powerful communication, and can be mastered when combined with the classics and a daily routine of paragraphs, essays and later more advanced work.

This is how real education takes place. You study and read and write; so does the student. Then you discuss and talk about it and see how it applies to real life and important questions and ideas; you read classics, books worth rereading, from all topics of study. If you can't understand a particular math or science classic, get someone in the community to read it with you and help. Many individuals with such expertise are delighted to be asked to share and help train hungry young minds. You are the mentor, helping where you can and getting others to help where you are limited. Keep it simple: you don't need a fancy curriculum, just the greatest works of all time, some hard work by you and your student, and lots of discussion and feedback on their work.

7. You, Not Them

Set the Example. The best mentors are continually learning and pushing themselves. Read the classics. Study hard. This allows you to take the "agency" approach to teaching, to let your students have a say in what they study next. "What are we going to do today, son? What is our next classic?"

"Well, I've been thinking about . . ."

"Okay, I will commit to study it, ponder and think about it, and we'll discuss it." Then study hard, pay the price in your own study, and require quality work from the student. A great mentor is not only one who gives assignments, but also one who accepts them and thereby allows the student to begin practicing leadership. A key part of setting the example is letting the students take the lead as often as possible; free choice is an essential part of learning to think.

George Wythe studied as hard as Jefferson, and Jefferson contacted him with questions and for help through his life until he passed away. The mentor must lead the way, by reading what the student reads, discussing it with him and requiring quality work.

In our modern society, whenever education is the subject, we always want to talk about the kids. We care about them, and we know their education is important, but we also find that it's easier to talk about their education than to improve our own. In reality, you are unlikely to pass on to your children a better education than you have earned yourself, no matter how much you push them or how good the teachers are in their private school. Children tend to rise to the educational level of their parents, and maybe a little above if their parents have shown them that this is important. The most effective way to ensure the quality of their education is to consistently improve your own.

The beauty of this self-evident truth is that you don't have to be all that far ahead of them to effectively lead out; they can even pass you up once you are firmly on a committed path of self-education. Your trajectory will propel them, even as the advantages of their youth and the time available to them allow them to achieve amazing amounts in a short period of time. Don't forget that you also have the advantage of maturity and life experience that enrich your learning in ways that they can't approximate. Just make the commitment and lead out. You be the lever that moves their world.

When you are setting the example, learning lessons and sharing them, you will be doing the most important thing you can to improve your children's education. This is equally true of parents and teachers.

Apply Lessons to Life

The most powerful lessons occur where studies intersect with real life. Mentors must constantly have students involved in applying the things they are learning. George Wythe had Jefferson and his other students attend the Virginia parliament, court cases, and other events and then discuss the similarities and differences between current events and the writings of the classics. Thomas Jefferson was present the day Patrick Henry gave his "Give me Liberty or Death" speech, and it had a major impact on him; it is likely he discussed it with his mentor. George Wythe also used the newspaper and pamphlets, the primary media of the day, as a source of comparison and application of Jefferson's study of the classics.

Mentors can help students get involved in the community in many ways, but most of this application comes during discussions of how the readings apply to real life. For example, consider how you could apply the lessons learned in *Jane Eyre*.

Jane Eyre is a story of a disadvantaged girl whose dreams finally come true, when all of a sudden at the very last minute before she is to be married, she finds out the man is already married. He tries to convince her it is appropriate due to the circumstances. But she knows it is wrong, absolutely wrong, and she leaves. She ends up begging for food on the street, going door-to-door asking for help, her clothes are worn out, she is totally exhausted. All she has to do is go back and accept this man's offer, and she'll be rich and have the man she loves. But she knows there is a clear right and wrong, and she chooses the right regardless of the consequences.

There is a lot of discussion that can take place in a family or classroom about this. Mom or Dad can say: "Let me tell you about our courtship and talk about some related ideas. While we're on the subject, let's talk about courtship as opposed to dating and look at the differences, and let's consider how it differs between those days and today." Teachers can deal with similar themes— right and wrong, and so on.

This works very well for current events. When you're watching World News Tonight, you might say, "That's an interesting take on it. We just got done reading Marx's *Communist Manifesto* and Madison in the *Federalist Papers*. Which of those viewpoints is this anchorman closest to in his thinking?" If your student says, "He's clearly Madison." You respond, "Why? Explain it to me." Then you talk it through. If you or your student are still unclear, go back to the books and make a list of, say, seven main ideas from both. Then you watch the news together for the next two weeks and take notes, and discuss it again. Then the student writes about it and you discuss what he or she has written. The whole time you're inspiring thought and leadership because the student learns how to think and how to apply what he is learning.

In addition, there are many ways to get out of the classroom and apply what students are learning—a family or class service project, family business, political campaigns, community or church service, travel, field trips, etc.

Almost any important subject you can think of is brought up in the classics; all you do is read them along with the student, discuss them together, and point out how they apply to the student personally and to current events—just like Wythe taught Jefferson: classics, discussion, writing, application.

Let me recap. The greatest leaders in history used a very simple curriculum. They read the classics, they discussed them with a mentor who accepted only quality work, and they applied what they learned to real life. The more we move away from this time-proven curriculum, the less successful we'll be in educating people and training leaders. Greatness is fostered by coming face-to-face with greatness, both in mentors and classics. Much of who Jefferson was he owed to the effort and direction of George Wythe. Much of who Abraham Lincoln was came as a result of his lifelong passion of studying one man: George Washington. He read the classics, many times by firelight. He discussed them with his mentors, the first of whom was his stepmother.

If you want to be successful in creating leadership education, in preparing students to lead their families, communities and careers, teach them how to think. How? Get them into the classics, do it with them, accept only quality, and apply it to real life. Over and over and over again until they leave your home or classroom. When they leave and go away to college or career, they'll be leaders. And so will you.

CHAPTER FIVE

Classics

*"It is chiefly through books that we enjoy intercourse with
superior minds.... In the best books, great men talk to us,
give us their most precious thoughts, and pour their souls into ours."*

—William Ellery Channing

*"How many a man has dated a new era in his life
from the reading of a book."*

—Henry David Thoreau

*"When you reread a classic you do not see more in the book than
you did before; you see more in you than was there before."*

—Clifton Fadiman

Please take out a blank sheet of paper. Now answer each of the following questions:

1. What books are your companions through life?

2. If you were evacuated to another planet and could only take one book, upon which to base the whole teaching of your family and establishing right and wrong for your community, what would it be?

3. What is good? What is evil?

I'll refer to these later, so please be sure to stop reading and answer these three questions in writing before continuing.

In 1987, the bicentennial of the Constitutional Convention, three very important best sellers swept America: Robert Bork's *The Tempting of America*, E.D. Hirsch's *Cultural Literacy*, and *The Closing of the American Mind* by Allan Bloom. They presented essentially the same message, about law, society, and education respectively: that we have strayed from our founding—and not in a good direction. In fact, together they are a sort of update to Tocqueville's *Democracy in America*.

Consider Allan Bloom's profound analysis of American education. As I read this modern classic, three major points stood out. First, societies are successful when people choose to be good. If people choose mediocrity, they end up with a mediocre society. If they choose excellence, they build an excellent society; if they choose decadence, society decays. This is not only common sense, it is historically accurate.

Second, people choose to be good when they are taught and believe in good. People's choices are a direct result of their beliefs. And their beliefs are profoundly influenced by what they are taught by parents, friends, teachers, clergy, etc. If they are taught a falsehood or even evil, and if they believe it, they will choose poorly. Teaching influences belief, which guides action.

Third, the thing which determines how well they are taught is their national books. A national book is something that almost everyone in the nation accepts as a central truth. The national book of the Jews is the Torah; Muslims, the Koran; Christians, the Bible; etc. It could be argued that Shakespeare is a national author for England, Goethe and Luther for Germany, Dante and Machiavelli for Italy, Tolstoy in Russia, and so on. Whatever the nation, its national books, the books almost everyone in the nation revere and believe in, will determine the culture. Good national books, like the Bible or Shakespeare's works, will lead to a good nation. Bad national books like *The Communist Manifesto* or *Mein Kampf* will lead to bad nations until they reject such books.

Now, what of a nation with no national book, with no central text which almost everyone agrees upon as the measuring rod of right and wrong? Such a nation is simply without culture, or at best it is in the process of losing it.

America's National Books

This leads to the question, "What is America's national book?" Bloom argues that when he was teaching college at the University of Chicago in the 1950s and 60s, he could tell what the national books were by asking students what books formed the core of their lives, the basis of society. The two answers he always got were the Bible and the *Declaration of Independence*. In the late 1960s this changed: Bloom's students really couldn't answer his question. They stopped referring to the Bible and the Declaration, and they listed…nothing. No national books. The Bible and the Declaration remained for the older generations, but the youngsters came up with no core source of absolutes, no central fountain of truth.

In the 1980s it changed again: students began listing various rock n' roll music artists as the thing they revered and turned to for truth and answers. Practically every college student knew this new fountain of truth, studied it daily and for long hours, and felt passionately about it. If you doubt it, Bloom suggested, try to tell a group of youth why their music is bad and they will respond with the same energy and even anger as if you had tried to tell a group 100 years ago that the Bible was bad.

This obviously could have some very negative ramifications for America's future, but even rock music isn't truly a national book because it is only shared by the younger generations.

In fact, there is no true national book in America today. No national books means no culture; and this is ominous for the future. Any society which loses its national book declines and collapses in ignorance, dwindles and perishes in unbelief. In Bloom's own words: "The loss of the gripping inner life vouchsafed those who were nurtured by the Bible must be primarily attributed not to our schools or political life, but to the family, which, with all its rights to privacy, has proved unable to maintain any content of its own...The delicate fabric of the civilization into which the successive generations are woven has unraveled, and children are raised, not educated...

"People sup together, play together, travel together, but they do not think together. Hardly any homes have any intellectual life whatsoever, let alone one that informs the vital interests of life. Educational TV marks the high tide for family intellectual life.

"The cause of this decay of the family's traditional role as the transmitter of tradition is the same as that of the decay of the humanities: nobody believes that the old books do, or even could, contain the truth.... In the United States, practically speaking, the Bible was the only common culture, one that united simple and sophisticated, rich and poor, young and old, and...provided access to the seriousness of books. With its gradual and inevitable disappearance, the very idea of such a total book and the possibility and necessity of world-explanation is disappearing. And fathers and mothers have lost the idea that the highest aspiration they might have for their children is for them to be wise—as priests, prophets or philosophers are wise. Specialized competence and success are all that they can imagine."[21]

Bloom is not only correct about the failure of the American family to fulfill its role as the primary center of education, his analysis of the modern famine of classics as the source of education is equally important: "My grandparents were ignorant people by our standards, and my grandfather held only lowly jobs. But their home was spiritually rich because all the things done in it, not only what was specifically ritual, found their origin in the Bible's commandments, and their explanation in the Bible's stories and the commentaries on them, and had their imaginative counterparts in the seeds of the myriad of exemplary heroes. My grandparents found reasons for the existence of their family and the fulfillment of their duties in serious writings, and they interpreted their special sufferings with respect to a great and ennobling past. Their simple faith and practices linked them to great scholars and thinkers who dealt with the same material.... There was a respect for real learning, because it had a felt connection with their lives. This is what a community and a history mean, a common experience inviting high and low into a single body of belief....

"Without the great revelations, epics and philosophies as part of our natural vision, there is nothing to see out there, and eventually little left inside. The Bible is not the only means to furnish a mind, but without a book of similar gravity, read with the gravity of the potential believer, it will remain unfurnished."[22]

If Bloom is correct, and I think he is, then America cannot remain free, prosperous or moral unless the overall culture adopts a central text of the caliber of the Bible. This is not only profound, it is actually a marching order for parents and educators. The whole problem is a result of families failing to teach, educate, train and civilize.

Study the Classics

This is the fundamental reason for studying the classics. We need a national book to maintain our morality and civilization; and a nation that doesn't regularly read good books, think about important ideas, or consider the big picture, is not capable of adopting or following a national book. National books must be carefully studied, pondered, discussed and talked about by a large portion of the population, or they lose their value and impact. We must read the classics, and families must lead out, or we will cease to be the kind of nation that deserves success, prosperity, civilization or happiness.

This may seem too dramatic, but the reality is that Greece, Rome, Egypt, Israel and other great civilizations in history fell the same way, following a similar pattern. We may think we are above that; so did they. We are not above it; nobody ever was nor ever will be; that is the message of the Bible, and it is only in a post-Bible America that we think otherwise. Our freedoms can be lost, and it is only in a post-*Declaration of Independence America* that we doubt it.

In addition to maintaining our freedom and our civilization, there are at least six other reasons to study the classics:

1. The Classics Teach us Human Nature

A knowledge of human nature is the key to leadership. There are four basic instincts which all humans have:

A. Survival and security
B. Social mobility, power, relationships
C. Adventure, excitement
D. To gain meaning; to know self, truth and God

The classics give us a glimpse into each of these basic human instincts. In fact, the thing which makes a classic great is glaring insight into basic human nature. Ultimately, as you study the classics, you learn about your own personal nature. Learning through experience is good, but it is often better to learn from someone else's experiences and build on them—we hope a baby will learn from his parents not to touch a hot stove, even though the actual experience would certainly have impact. If we will let them, the classics can teach us lessons without the pain of repeating certain mistakes ourselves. They can show us correct choices which will get us where we want to go.

We will certainly get our own share of challenging experiences, but learning from others can help us immeasurably on our journey. Classics allow us to experience, in an intimate way, the greatest mistakes and successful choices of human history. If we learn from these mistakes and successes, we will make fewer mistakes and have more successes.

At a deeper level, knowing how others think, feel and act allows us to predict behavior and lead accordingly. We can develop empathy, compassion, wisdom and self-discipline without subjecting our relationships to a more painful learning curve. This is invaluable to the entrepreneur, parent, community leader or statesman. People with experience have been through certain patterns many times and know what to anticipate. The classics can provide us with many such experiences.

2. The Classics Bring us Face-to-Face with Greatness

The purpose of studying literature is to *become* better. As we read we experience despair, heartache, tragedy—and we learn to recognize what causes them and avoid it or cope with it in our own lives. As we study the characters, real or fictional, in the classics, we are inspired by greatness, which is the first step to becoming great ourselves. Greatness is the first goal of leadership education.

In the classics we come face-to-face with Moses on Sinai, Buddha leaving the castle, Christ at Gethsemane, Mohammed's cave (and Plato's), Paul on Mars Hill, Adam's finger outstretched on the ceiling of the Sistine Chapel, Washington at Valley Forge, Hamlet, Lear, Shylock, Othello, Macbeth, MacDuff, Hector, Penelope and Jane Eyre. *Who we are* changes as we set higher and higher standards of what life is about and what we are here to accomplish.

3. The Classics Take us to the Frontier to be Conquered

All generations before this one have had geographical frontiers to conquer. We don't. Without a frontier we cannot become what the Founders, the explorers and the pioneers became in their extremities. Our challenges define us, our reactions to them mold and shape us. As Thucydides said over three thousand years ago, and as I like to tell my students at George Wythe College: "There is no need to suppose that human beings differ very much one from another: but it is true that the ones who come out on top are the ones who have been trained in the hardest school."[23]

Human beings need a frontier in order to progress. Fortunately, we do have one frontier left, and it is in fact the hardest one. It is the frontier within. In all of history, this frontier has not been fully conquered. The most challenging struggles of life are internal—and the classics can help.

The classics deal with the real questions of life, our deepest concerns: joy, pain, fear, love, hate, courage, anger, death, faith, and others. These issues are reality; they are eternal and more lasting than jobs, careers, school, or material things.

In the classics we can often experience other people's characters more powerfully than in real life because the author lets us see their thoughts, feelings and reasons for—and consequences of—their choices (which we hardly ever see in others, and often not even in ourselves). Our goal in life is to become truly good and really happy. The classics help us see that quest in others and how their choices fail or succeed. A by-product of this rapport is the erasure of prejudices and ill-founded biases that divide and factionalize us from others. Classics help us connect with individuals whatever their race, creed, age, culture and even place in history.

I fear that modernity has come to mean ignoring what is important because we are too busy with what is immediate.[24] Nietzsche said that the difference between modern and ancient times is that modern man substitutes the morning newspaper for morning prayer. Bloom adds that now we have replaced the newspaper with the television. Too often we focus on the mortal rather than the eternal; this is a disease of modern times.

The classics are a remedy and can be a cure. They force us to turn off the TV and computer, to quietly study for hours and hours and hours—reading, pondering, thinking, asking, crying, laughing, struggling, and above all, feeling, changing, becoming. And then, because we are better, we must go out and serve.

4. The Classics Force us to Think

First, we are caused to think about the characters in the story, then about ourselves, then about people we know and finally about humanity in general. At first reading the classics can be a chore, an assignment. If we persist, it eventually becomes leisure and even entertainment. Then one day (after a few weeks for some, perhaps years for another) something clicks; all the exposure to greatness reaches critical mass, and you, the reader, awaken. Your exposure to greatness changes you: your ideas are bigger, your dreams wilder, your plans more challenging, your faith more powerful.

The classics can be hard work, and that is exactly what is needed to learn to think. Thinking is hard; deep thinking is not entertaining or easy. Thinking is like exercise, it requires consistency and rigor. Like barbells in a weightlifting room, the classics force us to either put them down or exert our minds. They require us to *think*. Not just in a rote memory way, either. The classics make us struggle, search, ponder, seek, analyze, discover, decide, and reconsider. As with physical exercise, the exertion leads to pleasing results as we metamorphose and experience the pleasure of doing something wholesome and difficult that changes us for the better.

5. The Classics Connect Us to Stories

Each culture is different because it has different shared stories. Different stories define each family, each religion, each nation. And members of each connect *themselves* with the stories—they make the stories part of their personal story.

Can you imagine the Jews without the stories of Moses, the Maccabees, or the Holocaust? Or Americans without stories of Paul Revere, George Washington, and Abraham Lincoln? Learn the stories of a culture, and you will come to understand that culture. That is why I think it is such a tragedy that the current generation of American youth are mostly growing up without the stories of the *Declaration of Independence*, Daniel in the Lion's Den, Patrick Henry, Sitting Bull or Daniel Webster. The classics are the ark, the preserver, of stories which unite the cultures and the generations.

In addition to cultural, national and family stories, we each have individual stories. We all have a personal canon, a set of stories which we hang onto and believe in and base our lives around; and great classics are the best canon. A canon is the set of books we consider to be the standard of truth. Since the purpose of reading, of gaining education, is to become good, our most important task is to choose the right books. Our personal set of stories, our canon, shapes our lives. I believe it is a law of the universe that we will not rise above our canon. Our canon is part of us, deeply, subconsciously. And the characters and teachings in our canon shape our characters—good, evil, mediocre, or great.

6. Our Canon Becomes our Plot

There are four types of stories: bent, broken, whole, and healing.[25]

A. *Bent* stories portray evil as good, and good as evil. Such stories are meant to enhance the evil tendencies of the reader, such as pornography and many horror books and movies. The best decision regarding Bent stories is to avoid them like the plague.

B. *Broken* stories portray accurately evil as evil and good as good, but evil wins. Something is broken, not right, in need of fixing. Such books are not uplifting (in the common sense of the word), but can be transformational in a positive way. Broken stories can be very good for the reader if they motivate him or her to heal them, to fix them. *The Communist Manifesto* is a broken classic; so are *The Lord of the Flies* and *1984*. In each of these, evil wins; but they have been very motivating to me because I have felt a real need to help reverse their impact in the real world.

C. *Whole* stories are where good is good and good wins. Most of the classics are in this category, and readers should spend most of their time in such works.

D. *Healing* stories can be either Whole or Broken stories where the reader is profoundly moved, changed, or significantly improved by her reading experience.

I recommend three rules in coming face-to-face with greatness through the classics:

1. Avoid Bent stories.

2. Develop a personal canon of Healing stories.

3. Spend the majority of your studies in Whole works, but don't neglect Broken stories that you ought to be fixing.

Your National Book

Now, refer to the answers you wrote at the beginning of the chapter. Look at question number two: "If you were evacuated to another planet and could only take one book, upon which to base the whole teaching of your family and establishing right and wrong for your community, what would it be?"

Your answer is a good indication of what *your* national book might be.

Look at the other two answers you gave. Are your companion books through life in line with your national book? What about your definitions of good and evil? Look at your life; is it in keeping with your canon?

All of this can be very powerful as you analyze where to take the education of your children, your students, yourself. Perhaps the most important thing America can do to remain free and prosperous is to clarify a national book and live by it. From the Founding through the end of World War II, the Bible and the Declaration were our national books. Even the great revolutions which occurred after 1945, such as increased freedom for minorities, were fueled by these two national books. Martin Luther King, Jr.'s speeches center around them and quote them extensively. America was based on them and became what it did because of them. Take them away, and America will become something very, very different.

The place to start is with yourself. Establish a clear canon and spend time in it every day. Become an expert on it, ponder it, put your life in line with it. Teach it to your family and then others. If you are a teacher, take it into your classroom. If your faith doesn't include the Bible, use the Declaration or something of equal magnitude. Then broaden your knowledge to the other classics which support that central classic. America is what it is due to its national books, and the choices you make now regarding books will have tremendous impact on what America will be twenty, forty and even sixty years from now.

CHAPTER SIX

Great Teaching

"Think of a human pair teaching their child how to walk. There is, on the child's side, strong desire and latent powers: he has legs and means to use them. He walks and smiles; he totters and looks alarmed; he falls and cries. The parents smile throughout, showering advice, warning, encouragement and praise. The whole story, not only of teaching, but of man and civilization, is wrapped up in this first academic performance...."

"All the knowledge, skill, art, and science that we use and revere, up to Einstein's formulas about the stars, is a mere repetition and extension of the initial feat of learning to walk. But this extension does not take place by itself. Most of it has to be taught, slowly and painfully. There was a time when Einstein was not quite sure what eight times nine came to. He had to learn, and to learn he had to be taught."
—Jacques Barzun

A s we discussed earlier, education occurs when students set out to educate themselves and follow through. This happens when great teaching is present—either in mentors or classics, or both. The roles of students and teachers are clearly identified in the quotation above. Students educate themselves through the following process:

1. Observe others and identify a desired trait or skill to be acquired.

2. Walk and smile: try and have mini-successes.
3. Totter and look alarmed: run into difficulties and get worried.
4. Fall and cry: fail and feel bad.
5. Start over again.

As students go through this process over and over—trying, succeeding and failing, trying again—they become educated. All effective learning in any subject follows this format. The student must be the primary educator because the student will only learn, *can* only learn, what he *chooses* to learn.

Good teaching also follows a predictable format:

1. Smile throughout
2. Shower advice
3. Warn
4. Encourage
5. Praise
6. And, most importantly, set the example

Teachers teach, and when they do it well, students educate. This is at the center of all learning and is the key to success in any and every educational endeavor.

So far I have argued the following: that students must educate, indeed that they are the only ones who can effectively educate; that they will do so if they are taught by great teachers; that we should therefore focus on great teaching instead of educational problems; that great teachers come in two formats—classics and mentors; and that there are seven keys to great teaching.

As I give seminars around the nation, these themes seem to resonate with the majority of those who attend. But the number one question that parents and teachers ask is: "But how do I actually do it?" People ask this question after the first seminar they attend and after the second or third time. Many who have applied the classics/mentors model for more than a year still ask the same question.

"But How Do I Actually Do It?"

On the one hand, it is good to ask this question because even the best teachers should always seek improvement. For example, Judy Naegle, a former literature teacher in an excellent charter school, Heritage Academy in Mesa, Arizona, attended a Teacher Training seminar at George Wythe College each summer for many years and came each time with new challenges and concerns. She is one of the best teachers I know, and she was constantly seeking to improve—and therefore her students improved their own educational endeavors. I hope that none of us stop asking this question.

On the other hand, it concerns me that very often the person asking the question is not just seeking improvement, but really believes that teaching must somehow be more complex, that there must be a trick to it. This is a residual or side effect from the conveyor belt, a trust in experts and the idea that education must be complex to be good.

One of the inherent problems with the professorial (as opposed to mentorial) approach to teaching is that the first lesson learned is: "He is the expert; I am the child, the ignorant one." Degree of knowledge becomes identity—the child has no trust nor respect for the process of learning, because he is seldom familiarized with the process the teacher went through. There is a well-guarded mystique that the teacher somehow just "knows" and a chosen gnostic few will someday "get it." Most students never witness the labor the master has gone to nor are they schooled in the processes that bring expertise and mastery. The student learns to label himself, "I'm just no good at math," or "singing," as if it were good justification for never applying himself.

The mentor who shares her love for learning and willingness to submit to the labor that is the process of acquiring mastery, will communicate the value of persevering through difficulties and trusting that ignorance and confusion must ultimately give way to knowledge and understanding.

In fact, education is very, very simple. Teachers set the example by reading, pondering, writing about and discussing classics, and sharing their loves, interests and ideas with students. And students get inspired, go to work, find the study difficult and go back to the teacher for encouragement. When they get it, they return to the difficult process of learning. Learning is difficult, but the process is not complex.

In a seminar, right about now I would likely be hearing the question again: "But how do I actually do this?"

Almost every time people ask this specific question, they are either happy with the process and just want to improve, or they are struggling with the process *because they aren't personally reading the classics*. Consider a typical dialogue:

"But how do I actually do it?"
"How are you doing it now?"
"Well, he reads lots of books, many of them classics."
"Do you read them too?"
"Well, some of them."
"Okay, which ones have you read this month?"

This question is usually followed by a nervous silence, then:

"Okay, I know the classics thing. But how do we really make this work?"

"You read the classic. Your student reads the classic. You discuss it. He writes a report on it and you discuss it together. He gives an oral report to the class or family and you discuss that. You get other classmates or family members to read it and you meet for a group discussion. But of course none of this works unless you read it."

"But, what about things like math?"

"Exactly the same. I assume you are asking me because a student of yours is struggling with math, right?"

"Right. He reads classics and lots of things but I can't get him to read math classics."

"What was the last math classic or textbook that you read?"
"Uh…"

Almost nobody has an answer for this. If you haven't read math classics, it's almost impossible to teach math through the classics.

Teachers teach and students educate. Teachers teach by setting the example. If you want him to read math classics, you better start reading. Or get him working with someone who does. Students choose to educate themselves when they are inspired by teachers. If you don't read math classics, how can you inspire him to read them? You can't.

The answer to the question, "How do I actually do it?" is that you *get started*. You don't have to be an expert to teach well, you don't have to have a degree or years of experience teaching the subject, but you do have to read the classics, get excited about them, and pass on your enthusiasm and new knowledge to the student. At the very least, you can put the classics on the shelves of your home or in a prominent place in your classroom. Many homes don't even have a math classic (scripture excepted), much less a parent who reads it and shares what they are learning. For some students, just the presence of the book will be enough to get them started. But for most, the example of a parent or teacher who is reading, pondering, sharing and discussing is necessary. How do you actually do it? You pick up a book, turn to the first page, start reading, and share what you learn.

Start with books that will do much of the work for you, novels or biographies or others that are interesting and not terribly difficult. You can build up to the challenging books, but start with good books instead of great and follow up with lots of discussion about what you are learning. For example, to continue the math analogy, don't start with Newton or Einstein but something like *The Chosen* or *Gulliver's Travels*. When you come to the math sections, slow down and figure them out, and discuss them with your student before going on. In the context of trying to understand these very interesting novels, almost everyone will enjoy pulling out paper and pencil to work through the math. It will be difficult, but fun at the same time. Similar math classics for beginners might include *Flatland* by Edwin Abbot or *On Numbers* or the *Foundation* trilogy by Isaac Asimov, and a good book for parents is *Mathematics for the Millions* by Lancelot Hogben.

This gets at the heart of the matter, the reason people wonder if there isn't some complex system to follow. Really, the only complex part of it is knowing enough books to be able to recommend where to start and where to go next. I have tried to get you started with this book. Once you get through the first few months, it is just a matter of continually expanding your own education and inviting your student(s) along for the ride.

The Five Environments of Mentoring

Once parents and teachers begin this process, their question changes to: "How can I improve my teaching?" At this point, consider how well you are using the Five Environments of Mentoring: tutorial, group discussion, lecture, testing and coaching. A good mentor-teacher incorporates them all into an overall package, helping inspire the student to consistently new breadths and depths of self-education.

Tutorial

Tutorials consist of a teacher and 1-6 students discussing something they have all read. Tutoring is not, as conveyor belt education has come to use it, simply lecturing to one or a few students. It is a discussion, and all who attend should come prepared. You can only tutor something you have yourself read and thought about, and it only works in a small group. The fewer the number, down to a minimum of the teacher and one student, the more depth you can go into in the discussion. Still, the best tutorials are often experienced with 4-7 people involved in the discussion or project.

Tutoring is the first form of teaching, and at its highest level it incorporates two people talking about a great classic and how it applies to their lives in real and important ways. The two talk as equals, neither as the expert, but both as human beings seeking truth and knowledge in order to live better lives and be better people. Also, tutoring a student who is behind on the conveyor belt is very different than leadership tutorial.

Group Discussion

Group discussions are like tutorials, but with 6-30 people. Some of my most meaningful educational experiences have come in group discussions about classics arranged with faculty members, a group of students, combined classes, family members, or several homeschool families. A variety of books and group discussion formats can be followed at the same time. For example, within thirty days of writing the first edition of this book our family was involved with homeschool group discussions of *Sackett's Land, Anne of Green Gables,* and *Black Beauty.* Parents attended all of them, and participated but were careful not to dominate in any way. We also, during this same time period, held two group discussions just for parents, one on *Cheaper by the Dozen* and the other on *Uncle Tom's Cabin.*

As with tutorials, group discussions should be led by a guide, one who calls on raised hands to speak and otherwise moderates the discussion. Guides must avoid the urge to turn the discussion into a lecture or soapbox, but they must also open up and share while leaving most of the time to the students. Usually this requires the patience to let things remain silent for a minute, or perhaps as much as fifteen minutes. Eventually, if the adults refuse to give up, students will open up and talk—and it is nearly always worth the wait.

Lecture

Lecture is the most overdone of the five environments in most school settings, but it is very valuable when done well. Lecture consists of one person talking while the students take notes, with perhaps a few minutes for questions and answers at the end. This is not the best form of teaching unless the lecturer is truly an expert and her time with the students is necessarily short. Most parents should avoid lecture just as most classroom teachers should avoid it; better to guide the student through self-discovery than to just tell them what you think they should know.

Bringing in outside experts to share their ideas and experiences can be wonderfully inspiring and helpful to both teacher and student. In our home, for example, we engaged the expertise of a George Wythe College math instructor with a real gift for helping students understand and love math, and we opened his two-month course to other homeschoolers. Our son came away thrilled about math, enthusiastically telling stories about Archimedes, and memorizing square roots. At George Wythe College, we have periodic visiting formal lectures; almost everything else emphasizes the other four environments.

Testing

Testing has a bad name for many people due to the conveyor belt, but it is an important part of teaching if done correctly. Different kinds of tests evaluate different things, and perhaps most tests have value in some setting. Two types of exams really help teachers teach and students self educate: essays and orals.

One purpose of exams is to test the student's acquisition of knowledge and ability to communicate and apply it. The real question is: "Has he learned to think?" Multiple choice, fill-in-the-blank, and other such exams measure memory of facts only, which requires little *thinking*. They may be valuable if they are not used as exams at all, but as surveys at the beginning of instruction followed by discussion. Such exams should only be given where the instructor wants to emphasize detailed fact retention; even in such cases, it is usually better to ask essay questions which require precise detail. Of course, it is probably valuable for older students to become proficient in such exams and their methods as practical preparation for life.

Exams should usually be done from memory; open book exams are really papers or projects. Essay exams measure memory of fact, ability to organize and express, application and persuasion, and allow for high levels of personal feedback from the teacher.

The key is time and feedback: good teachers don't just grade exams, they sit down with the student after the fact and use them to discuss and teach. Students often perform better, indeed learn and think better, when they are told well in advance exactly what to expect on written exams, particularly when an extreme amount is expected.

Students should also be given the freedom to propose alternatives to teacher exams; teachers have full authority to accept or reject proposals, and should be fair and quality-oriented.

Oral exams are a very important teaching and learning setting. They have all the benefits of essay exams, plus they add the dimension of public performance, thinking on one's feet, and persuading verbally.

Both essay and oral exams can be done informally or formally. Informal is usually best for younger students. For example, a test may be as simple as having students write down everything they remember at the end of each study day or asking them questions about what they've covered.

The important thing to remember is that testing is valuable when done right—when the mentor and student sit down after the exam and discuss, debate, reconsider and coach. Almost any type of exam is helpful with such follow up.

Coaching

Remember the parents coaching the toddler learning to walk? The coaching teacher, the caring, nurturing guide is the proper model for great teaching. This applies all through the academic parts of learning—tutorials, group discussions, exams and even lectures (where the mentor discusses student reaction to the lecturing expert). The coach stays on the sidelines, teaches, demonstrates, watches the student try and then responds.

Coaching is also essential in the non-academic, that is, *applied* part of a student's education. Coaches arrange field trips, apprenticeships, music or other types of lessons, simulations or internships, church or community service projects, Scouting or athletic involvements and other opportunities for growth and learning. Of course, many opportunities arise without the coach's nudging.

All of these, and most importantly, just the ups and downs of everyday life, are opportunities for coaching, discussing right and wrong or alternative options and chances for mentorial counsel and guidance.

The purpose is to help students educate themselves, to become happy, able and responsible human beings—and coaching is vital to the process. Indeed, coaching occurs one way or the other, even if just by bad example or ambivalence.

Taken together, the five environments of mentoring empower a teacher to do his/her job, which is to inspire self-education and help students follow through. Each of these five environments really is as simple as I have made it sound.

Now let's consider how a mentor-teacher might apply these simple, though certainly challenging (because of the amount of study and work needed), methods to teach some basic subjects.

Teaching Writing

From the first time the students ask how to write their name or the letter "H," to their entrance essays for college and beyond, the teaching of writing follows the same model. Students write, teachers coach. You give feedback, ideas, comments, suggestions; they do it over and over until they do it well. Just like any other subject, you must model it. Write letters and thank-you notes, to them and to others, write summaries of ideas from your readings and share them with your students, and so on. They must see you writing and they must see you re-writing. Invite them to read the various drafts of your work so they can begin to internalize the labor that is required to dig a little deeper and do it again, to analyze critically what had seemed just fine only moments before, to toss away irrelevant content even when you like the way it sounds; then, when you ask them to write and rewrite, they at least know that you are asking them to do something that is valuable and important to you.

Dr. Andrew Groft, Provost at George Wythe College, teaches writing by assigning mini-papers. Students write their main ideas, and then their few main supporting ideas. The mentor coaches, asks questions, gives feedback. Then the student takes each idea and writes a mini-paper on it, and the mentor coaches each section.[26] As papers, creative works and other projects get longer and deeper, more feedback is required. Don't permit the student to attempt to write about something that doesn't interest her. This is a dead end of frustration and bad habits. Be in tune with the student's passions and interests, fears and dreams, and encourage and direct her to record them in prose.

At first, the mentor should emphasize feedback on content. Eventually, as the student's writing matures, mentors coach all aspects of the writing. As mentor, be aware that the intimate knowledge you have of your student's current level and limitations can prove an obstacle to the student's pursuit of excellence. Your efforts to correct spelling, grammar and punctuation may seem arbitrary to the student not naturally inclined to such attention to detail. In such cases, one may successfully appeal to the student's desire to be well thought of by seeking an audience for her work—some interested third party (a grandparent, neighbor, other students in a Discussion Group, etc.) whom the student would like to favorably impress with not only content, but presentation and refinement. In such situations, the need for attention to details is not only obvious to the student, but has very personal implications in terms of emotional rewards or embarrassments. Ultimately the student will gain a personal standard and should find inherent pleasure in saying what she means and saying it well. The passion to be understood is almost universal and the student who sees herself growing in effectiveness while expressing herself will likely do so more frequently and with greater skill.

This is key to good writing: students must be reading good writers. For example, I distinctly remember the feeling I had in one class on Tocqueville's *Democracy in America*; several students and I repeatedly marveled at his use of language, and I think each of us left the class dedicated to improving our writing.

Teaching Reading

In the Three R's, there are at least two levels of learning—literacy and mastery. Students first learn the techniques of basic reading, writing and ciphering, and then they master the abilities to read analytically and critically, write clearly and communicate effectively, and think mathematically. The teaching of both levels follows the familiar classics/mentor model: students see a mentor reading, work with a mentor reading to them, are inspired by example to try it themselves, succeed and are praised, fail and are encouraged and coached, and keep trying until they are literate. Then they repeat the process with serious books that require pondering, rereading, discussion, analysis, debate and more discussion.

In teaching a young child to read, there is no substitute for "lap reading." It is here that the mentorial trust, affection and desire to please are established and nurtured. It is here that through parent bonding and memorable moments a child gains a rapport with books as his friends and teachers, grows comfortable and familiar with the symbols of language on the page, gains a curiosity and drive to encounter the secrets of pages not yet turned, and ultimately the confidence that reading must be within his reach, for it has always been a part of his life, and his parents have not only mastered it but communicate in word and deed that he will too, in due time. A child that is read to consistently and often will not need to be pushed to learn to read.

It is extremely important that we not choose an arbitrary age at which a child must learn to read. My wife Rachel was an independent reader at age four; I was not until between ages nine and eleven. Our son, Oliver, was "slower" like me, though not quite as slow as I was. In his case, homeschooling was a great blessing; although at age nine he was conscious that most of his friends were more advanced in reading, he chose to orient himself by our lack of alarm and our confidence that his progress was appropriate and he would master reading, just as we did in our time. His younger sisters (Emma, Sara, and Eliza) came to reading more quickly, as their mother did. Our approach and involvement with each one's progress has been unique, owing to the varying levels of interest and our own parental instinct of what was best for their personal and collective development.

Another advantage of being patient with young Oliver's progress is he never got into the habit of being pushed by us, and as a result he has the innate sense that his education is his responsibility and his reward. We are his guides and facilitators, but the will to achieve must be his own. This greatly reduces the burden and stress on the parent and results in a superior and life-long pursuit of education and self-improvement. Today, as a fourteen-year-old, he is a voracious reader and an excellent student. He has taken several college classes, but is mostly still focused on his real areas of interest—math, science, and reading. He works a little on writing and a lot on social studies—and he loves to talk and discuss the thinking of Nietszche, Jung and Campbell. But nobody who knows him would think he's an egghead—he loves Scouts, karate, and sports.

Just as it is helpful to read lots of books to the child, the youth gains a great deal by reading passages of difficult classics or documents with the mentor, slowing down to clarify obscure text, stopping to look up vocabulary and pausing to discuss why a semicolon is used and how the meaning would change by inserting a period or dash. Like children's books, these kinds of reading tutorials are best accomplished in short but frequent doses.

Of course, like in all other subjects, the greater the book and the more caring and personalized the mentoring, the better the teaching environment. Most parents know the time and effort it takes a child to learn to walk; similar effort is required for most students to master analytical reading and most other subjects.

Teaching Literature

There are many different lists of classics, but there is no single "correct" list. Part of the power of the classics is that you have to study them for yourself and find out if they are truly *classic*.

The question I usually get asked at this point in the seminars is: "Will the students really get an education if all they study is literature?" But the question assumes that "classics" means literature. It doesn't. There are classics in every field. Name a field—it has classics, works worth studying over and over which provide glaring insight into human nature. Even in the most modern or technical fields there are classics. Literature is the easy one; we tend to equate the two because this is one field where our schools still use classics like Shakespeare, Dickens and Austen.

Teaching History

Plutarch, Gibbon, Toynbee, Durant. Have you heard of these authors? Have you read them? If not, they are a great start to your study of history. You must study if you plan to teach. In fact, that is what a school is: mature scholars studying and inspiring young scholars to do the same. Also, actual documents are very helpful. For example, if you want to teach about the American Revolution, read The *Declaration of Independence* together in tutorial or group discussion. Read the letters that the Founders wrote to each other about it, and newspaper articles from the time period. Journal entries are also very valuable. All of these can be classics. It takes some work to search them out, but they are so much more effective than textbooks.

Biography is one of the best methods of teaching history, especially if you can find biographers whose work fits the definition of classics. Students should really start with biography and historical fiction before moving on to facts, names, dates, etc. In fact, for several years at George Wythe College, our undergraduate history program was built on in-depth research of one historical individual per semester. The whole class studied the same person, including numerous biographies, letters, journals, newspaper and periodical accounts, etc. We still incorporate lots of biography into the curriculum along with the other classics of history. This accomplishes not only a sense of real understanding of the individual and how history is made, but trains the students in the techniques of research and presentation. This liberates them to undertake whatever course of study they choose, independent of teachers or textbooks. The classics bring depth, which translates into real breadth over time.

Teaching Math

If you really want to learn math, at all levels, read Euclid, Newton's *Principia Mathematica* and the other great mathematical classics of history including current thinkers.

Study the great mathematicians in the order they appeared, because they build upon each other. The mathematical discoveries of Archimedes are a great place to start. Of course, students still need to learn the principles of arithmetic, geometry, algebra, trigonometry and calculus, but all of these subjects were discovered and developed over time by the great mathematicians.

We have used this method at home, in our private K-12 school, Colesville Academy (which my wife founded), and at the college level. Dr. Troy Henke, an adjunct mentor at George Wythe College, has used it to teach classes to youth 8-16 and at the college level. He combined stories of great mathematicians, their original writings, and the re-creation of their problems and experiments, and the students excel. As Mr. Henke put it to the students: "Mathematics is an integral part of a statesman's education ....Math teaches a person to think in a way that no other field does. As a person studies math, he learns to:

1) seek and recognize patterns,

2) explore the relationship between things,

3) see similarities and also distinctions,

4) analyze logically but with a deep sense that there is a right answer and a set ideal worth detecting,

5) compare and contrast,

6) see things in black and white,

7) see infinite shades of grey and therefore avoid jumping to conclusions,

8) seek evidence for conclusions and check opinion with firsthand research,

9) put his own pen to paper before accepting what society tells him,

10) seek for absolutes,

11) remain open to surprising new information which makes past conclusions limited though perhaps still accurate....

"Now, clearly, the practical art must also be mastered—we want you to be able to pass any standardized test with the highest marks. But more importantly, we want you to be able to think like an Archimedes, a Descartes, a Newton, a Sophie Germain, an Einstein."[27]

The average improvement in one four-month semester of college students in this course, based on before and after sample nationalized tests, was a 22% increase in scores. The low was 18% and the high was 40%. This was not a scientific study, but our experience is that the system works. It does wonders for student enthusiasm about math, invites them to reassess their own math aptitude, helps the student see the relevance and importance of math, piques the interest and makes math part of their world. The question, "How will I ever use this in real life?" practically disappears.

Teaching Science

Copernicus, Galileo, Agassiz, Einstein. These men wrote volumes, they are among the greatest scientists ever, yet some science textbooks give us the random quote with a picture and a few lines of biography. When the greatest leaders in history, including Jefferson, wanted to study Newton, they read Newton. Anything else just dumbs us down. Newton is hard to read, I admit. That's one of the things that make it so great. One reason education has deteriorated in the past fifty years is that most of us don't take responsibility for our own education. We look for the easy way. If you are wondering how to get students to read Newton, you are asking the wrong question. The question is: Have you read

Newton? If you haven't, you've got some homework.

Children are natural-born scientists. They are explorers, inventors, artists, and philosophers. As a mentor you must be fluent in "the scientific method." Guide your students daily through the steps with Socratic self-restraint, and stay out of their way as they make sense of and draw meaning from the world around them. Reserve for them the moment of discovery as they seek answers to their questions. Perhaps most importantly, erase the lines between "science" and literature, art, music, math, language, culture and history. This may be very difficult for teachers in a formal school setting, but all students need to understand that science is all of these, and the cultivated mind is not only curious and active, but automatically detects the relationships between these commonly segregated fields of human experience.

Imagine the excitement of your student as he reads about the lives, questions, discoveries and accomplishments of the scientists of history and then duplicates their experiments to experience what they knew. Imagine your excitement as your student experiments on questions of his own to find undiscovered truths and new applications. As you and your student(s) learn from the great scientists of history, preferably in generally chronological order, eventually tackling the greatest scientific minds of humanity, and combine this study with lab experimentation and—as always—lots of discussion, you will not only learn many scientific facts and principles, you will also learn to think like scientists.

Note that the stories of great mathematicians and scientists are necessary to effectively teach math and science. For example, just imagine how difficult it would be to teach the concept of faith if you tried to do it without telling stories from the Bible or the lives of great men and women who used faith. It would be supremely, and unnecessarily, difficult. By sharing stories about Moses and the Red Sea, faith is grasped by even the youngest students. In contrast, most of our schools and parents have chosen to teach math and science without using the stories of the great mathematicians and scientists. This is a serious mistake. Some students will learn anyway, but many are frustrated by our short-sighted teaching techniques. I recommend reading the books *Scientists Who Changed the World, Mathematicians are People Too* and *Men of Mathematics*. Three other excellent works that introduce the connections of math and science to life are *The Pyramid Project* by Tiffany Rhoades Earl and Aneladee Milne, the Kimber Principle-Based math system, and *A Beginner's Guide to Reconstructing the Universe*, by Michael S. Schneider. Of course, nothing substitutes for the classics.

Teaching Foreign Language

Every language has its own classics. Do you want to learn Spanish? Read a great classic like *Don Quixote* in Spanish. If you want to learn Russian, read *War and Peace* in Russian. Perhaps most effective is to take a text already familiar to you—such as scripture—and read the target-language text concurrently with your native language text and a dictionary. You will find your dependence on the English text diminishes rapidly as your fluency increases. Jacques Barzun recommends a similar process with two dictionaries—a translation dictionary and a full dictionary in the target language.[28]

This method is the best and quickest way to learn it; when I say "quickest," I mean native-level, culturally rich comprehension and fluency. If you really want to teach students a language, simulate the way the native speakers learned it—in stories, in a shared tradition. The ideas that their parents talked about, the names they gave to things, and the stories they told *are* the language. Also helpful might be learning to tell fairy tales, favorite family stories, recite poems or scripture verses, sing children's songs in the target language, with particular attention to rhythm of speech and dramatic inflection. Stories can be told while drawing a primitive, easy-to-imitate illustration using a blend of English and the target language. Learn to pray or to conduct familiar daily routines in the target language. Master the vocabulary of a certain scenario, which can be utilized frequently, like: an apology, a request for help, giving directions, expressing appreciation, "good night" routines, etc.

Teach language through the classics and you'll automatically teach culture, international relations and diplomacy. Plus, the students will use it more fluently and richly than the textbook learners.

Teaching the Arts

Classics aren't just read, they are also painted, sculpted, constructed, and composed. The arts provide some of the most powerful classics. As with math, science and literature, have the students study the great masters, then practice composing, sculpting or painting their own work. Be positive as you coach your student in creating her art. For example: "I like the colors you chose!" "Tell me about your project," or, "What do you like best about it?" "What didn't turn out as you'd hoped?" "What techniques do you need to master to better express what you'd like to communicate?" Sometimes giving the child a different perspective—like displaying a sculpture high above eye level—will help her detect things worthy of attention (this is often better than making a point of it). As with writing, finding an audience for the student's work can greatly incentivize the pursuit of excellence.

Studying classics in visual arts is often best accomplished after the same pattern already described for math, science and even languages—art has a context in history as does every mathematical question; when the lives of the artists are illuminated in terms of world history, relevance and connectedness result. The student can identify with the artist and consider both the forces that led to the creation of the work and the effect it had artistically, politically, spiritually and societally on the audience.

As I talk of the holistic approach to teaching and learning, you may be wondering: "But who has time for this? If I go that in-depth with everything, I'll never get through it all by the time they are sixteen."

This raises a very important issue. One of the inherent problems with the conveyor belt format commonly used in public and most private and even homeschools is the arbitrary and inappropriate use of deadlines. The very message of "graduation" is misleading no matter how you slice it: 1) you'd better get your learning in by a certain date or it doesn't count; 2) you have somehow achieved in twelve years of conveyor belt-style experiences a wealth of knowledge worthy of endorsement by the state; 3) after twelve years you are a "finished product;" and 4) "Whew! You made it! Now you can quit learning!"

I honestly believe that if all you ever did during those years was to study art after the fashion just described, you would come away with a superior education, and more importantly, would feel not only the desire and the duty to continue, but would be totally confident in how to proceed. Of course, no parent wants to limit their child's education to just one topic, but studying the classics of all the great fields of human knowledge is the very definition of a real education. Everything else falls short.

This combination of the greatest human classics and hands-on experience is the essence of Jefferson Education. The arts are perhaps the most important because they deal in the medium of feeling and expressing. Writing comes before reading because most students, if left to their own devices, will ask how to write their name before they seek to learn to read. That is, self expression comes before the desire to study others. Art comes before writing. Children can be practicing artists before they study great art, and their studies will be the better for it.

Again, the method is simple. The teacher sets the example by practicing the art or studying the great painting or composition. Then he shares his enthusiasm and interest with the student. The student begins and the teacher coaches. They look at Picasso's work together and discuss it, they read his history and discuss it, and so on.

Teaching Other Subjects

All fields have classics. Business has the writings of Peter Drucker, Edward Demming and Stephen Covey; government has Locke, Madison and Tocqueville; psychology has William James, Freud and Skinner; biology has Hippocrates, Agassiz and Darwin.

Whatever the field, it contains classics. And if you don't like Freud or Darwin, study them in depth and know them better than their proponents. You'll often find that modern tradition mischaracterizes classics and historical figures to fit an agenda. Read the originals, draw your own conclusions and encourage your students to do likewise. Just like Jefferson did. Then you can really mentor your students.

Where a student sits geographically—in a public, private, or home classroom—does not determine which system he is in—conveyor belt, professional or leadership. The most important factor in determining the type of system is his teacher's goals and methods.

You can find superb mentors in almost all conveyor belt school districts and private schools. When I went to school, I had several such teachers. My fourth grade teacher was a mentor, and he emphasized the classics. We memorized about twenty poems during that year, spent a long section on music with him at the piano; and he read several classics to us during the year, ending each day with thirty minutes of reading to us. His grading was the "feedback" kind where he expected us to redo poor work; in a class of about thirty, he was a master at spending quality time with each student. This was in a public, conveyor belt school—but it was a Jefferson Classroom. The teacher was my own father.

In high school I had others, most notably Ms. Herrick's senior English. This was the hardest class I had ever taken up to that time; it was full of classics, writing and rewriting, engaging in real life community projects and lots of one-on-one mentoring. What a great teacher she was, a real mentor. Several other teachers were Jefferson quality mentors: Mr. Hill, Mr. Wood, Mr. Christensen and the Principal, Mr. Goulding. It seemed that he knew every student personally, how they were doing; he talked to me on many occasions about my studies, my interests and aspirations, and life in general. My own mother taught in my high school, and I took several Jefferson-style classes from her.

Forgive my stroll down memory lane, but I am sure that each of you can recall similar teachers in whatever system of school you attended. I'll bet that the teachers you really remember as mentors both challenged you academically and really cared about you personally.

My point is that using the public school doesn't mean you have to rely on the conveyor belt; just because you're homeschooling or enroll the kids in a private school doesn't mean you are off the conveyer belt. If you are still worried about curriculum and hidden secrets of teaching, chances are you still have one foot in the system. Go to work reading the classics yourself, invite your students along with you and have lots of discussions along the way. If you are already doing this, start structuring in tutorials, group discussions, visiting lectures, essay and oral exams and coaching.

Questions and Answers

Q: Newton and Einstein are pretty daunting. Is there any way to get them in a more readable form, with modernized language? Is that acceptable?

A: The reason they're in that form is because that's how Newton's brain worked and you need to know Newton's brain if you are going to truly understand the great ideas he was explaining. So don't get them in a more readable format; take them on. I don't necessarily recommend them first thing for beginners, however. Students can read the more basic things first and work up to it, but they aren't likely to do so unless you lead out.

Q: The vocabulary of the classics can be difficult. How do you help students through all the new vocabulary?

A. In science or math the vocabulary is just as difficult in textbooks as in classics (so is the writing style), so you might as well go to the great minds. I stop and talk to my students about words that they don't know. When I see their eyes sort of fuzz over, I stop and ask if they know what the words mean, then discuss them in context. Jefferson Education requires you to be an amateur etymologist, always researching the roots of words. If I gave you Newton's *Principia Mathematica* or even

Robinson Crusoe, do you think there might be words you wouldn't know?

[Answer: "Yes."]

What would you do with them?

[Answer: "Look them up in the dictionary."]

That's right, but in our society most people don't look them up. Most people skim right over them. Stop and look them up, and have your students do the same. Then discuss the word, its roots and connotations, etc. The goal is not, as Neal A. Maxwell put it, to get through the book, but rather to get the book through you. Slow down and learn, stop checking off assignments and start really digging, pondering, thinking. Ask the same of your students.

I recommend that every home have a copy of Noah Webster's 1828 dictionary, a current unabridged dictionary, and at least two word origin dictionaries for reference.

Q: What about memorizing? You seem to focus on reading and discussing and doing assignments, but what about things like times tables?

A: Rote memorization has value, but too often it is used to store the wrong kind of information and is overemphasized as an educational tool. Please don't jump to conclusions about what I am saying, one way or the other. It is easy to get caught in the trap of "rote memorization is bad so let's avoid it altogether," or at the other extreme, build a curriculum designed around cramming long lists of memorized data for the exam and then forgetting them within a few days or weeks. Neither extreme is good education.

Memorizing is a fabulous means of learning, particularly if the student is memorizing poetry or lines from plays or great classical works or speeches from historical figures. I recommend that you help students memorize a number of things they can use when they are speaking, performing or writing. As a mentor you can help them memorize this way, and it will be very valuable to them. And yes, the times tables need to be memorized along with things like the periodic table. But don't build your whole system around memorizing dry facts and testing them on things they'll soon forget. Find a balance here; use memorization only in a way that really helps them get a great education.

Q: Are you opposed to them getting the information from a more visual means, such as video, or listening to the classics on tape or CD?

A: Yes and no. There are classic videos, classic movies, classic music on tape. Use them. But classics come in a medium. Can you imagine teaching Picasso or Rembrandt by explaining it in a book without pictures? Or the same for Mozart or Bach with no listening? Or Shakespeare in pictures with no words? No: stick to the medium the classic came in. Newton presented his ideas in a book, so read it.

Now, listening to Newton and the other classics on tape can be a good supplement to the originals. I tell my students to listen to the tapes, watch the movies, read commentaries like Cliff Notes, and so on, but *in addition* to the originals, never in place of them. Approaching the classics from different media can stimulate creativity and thinking, so go for it. And in fact some works, like Shakespeare's plays, are originals both in writing and in performance. But always, always make sure you emphasize the original, whatever it is.

Q: You seem to leave out technology, the internet and all the learning programs available for computers. What is the role of technology in Thomas Jefferson Education?

A: Thoreau said: "We are in great haste to construct a magnetic telegraph from Maine to Texas; but Maine and Texas, it may be, have nothing important to communicate."[29] In many ways, this quote sums up our modern life. We think technology must be effective in education just because it exists, but the computers and the internet are just tools.

Tools can be very valuable in the hands of a master mechanic or carpenter, but unless he knows what he is doing the tool will at best get in the way and at worst could do real damage. Tools have specific uses; the computer is an excellent tool for writing, the internet good for certain kinds of research and communication, and educational software for entertainment and reinforcement. But none of them teach a student to think. Indeed, they are more likely to get in the way. I believe that letting students work on computers is about the same as putting them in front of a television—it can be entertaining, fun, and even educational if done with supervision and in small doses, but it is very easily abused and the people who try to justify it the loudest ("I just love the History Channel!" or, "It teaches good hand/eye coordination.") are usually over users.

When a student is ready to write extensively, the computer becomes a valuable tool; before that, it must not be allowed to stifle the difficult process of studying and learning to think.

Q: What about students who have been in public school for a long time and just don't want to read or learn anything?

A: Good. That gives you several months of a head start to begin reading the classics; you'll be that much more prepared when they decide to start learning. At some point you may need to help them jumpstart their education. All students are different, some of them will come around if you just leave them alone, others need you to set up some rules and enforce a disciplined routine.

In some more extreme cases where the children are older or are numerous, the social impact of getting off the conveyor belt can be extremely trying on the family. Most will transition effectively back through the Phases to get on track if a careful program of family activity is instituted which emphasizes wholesome activity that does not reward conformity but keeps the attention of the individuals. Some examples include hiking, hands-on art creation, service projects, travel, etc. When "detoxing" the family while getting off the conveyor belt, some time is required to rediscover family culture and unity, and the dynamic roles within the family. Children need to relearn sibling bonds and parents need to relearn their role as the primary caretakers.

Often the stress of doing this in the living room day after day can be wearing on one's resolve, and the negative baggage that comes is more than some are willing to bear. By over-programming family time with wholesome and constructive projects, the family can ease off the conveyor belt. This should be done in conjunction with an initially minimal and progressively expanding family routine, including the national book "devotional" and a few minutes in a classic each day. As the individuals in the family begin to relax into the security of the nest, this family routine can expand and the over-programming can decrease. Above all, seek inspiration and trust it.

There may be a time, initially, for a little bit of capriciousness just to entice your students to give learning a try. Affix rewards to their keeping commitments that are clearly over-generous on your part, and thus an act of charity rather than of payoff. Just remember that if you have to discipline them to study, discipline is discipline; it is not education. They may need discipline to start studying, but they absolutely must be inspired by good teaching if you want them to start learning. So get to work on the classics yourself, and then, depending on the student, pay the price to inspire him to get started also. This is very, very simple, but for many students it is not at all easy.

For formal classroom teachers, this can be even more difficult—but the same principles apply. Get them involved in class projects and start inspiring them to read the classics.

Q: But what if they just sit there?

A: Then you are probably only doing tutorial, lecture and coaching. Get some group discussions going and then be patient. For example, one private school teacher who took a George Wythe College Seminar went home and applied the TJEd system in her classroom. She assigned the students a classic, set a date for discussion, and told the students that this would be discussion instead of lecture. On the day of the discussion, the students sat for ten minutes with blank stares. Frustrated, she took over and gave a wonderful lecture on the value of the book, its relevance, and so on. This went on until the next seminar where she told me that the system just doesn't work. I told her to let the students give each other blank stares the entire class period. And the next one. And every one after that until they talked. And to tell them beforehand what she would be doing.

Of course, I am not saying that every study period should be done this way; lecture and discussion are necessary and valuable. But when you set aside a time for group discussion, don't turn it into a lecture. Be quiet. She tried it and things changed drastically. The class came alive, after several periods, and the students really opened up and began to *think* and to share.

While the students are getting off the conveyor belt, let them go through the needed transition. They don't really believe that you want them to think. You must prove it to them, and this takes patience.

Whatever you do, don't tell them you want them to think and then promptly attack their ideas once they open up. Be silent, bring them out, ask if anyone in the group has a response. If their ideas are way out, let the other students bring them back. Or wait a few weeks and bring the topic up in a discussion. But don't shut down the thinking process. In fact, do everything you can to reward it.

Q: How do I know where to start?

A: Don't try to get the "perfect" book or spend time making elaborate plans. Pick a book, haul it around wherever you go, and read it. If you struggle finding free time, start with a classic novel that is entertaining and sure to pull you in, like *Alas Babylon* or *The Lonesome Gods*. When you finish one, go to another. Create a habit of reading classics, take notes while you read them, and teach or discuss them afterwards. Or write about them.

If you just can't do this without external structure, assign the books you want to read to your students and give them a deadline and a date for discussion. This will force you to be prepared. Teaching is a great way to get an education, much more so than being a student. Turn your classroom or home into a Jefferson Classroom, and within a few years you will become the outstanding leader you want your students to be.

CHAPTER SEVEN

Thomas Jefferson Education in the Public Schools

You were born with potential.
You were born with goodness and trust.
You were born with ideals and dreams.
You were born with greatness.
You were born with wings.
You are not meant for crawling, so don't.
You have wings.
Learn to use them and fly.

—*Rumi*

"Ever before the teacher is a vision of the ideal student, the boy or girl equipped to study independently, intelligently, and with lofty purpose."

—*Bessie W. Stillman*

" ...the emphasis is placed on the absorption of as large an amount of material as possible, not on the understanding of the material; and on marks rather than on gain in power. If we are to produce citizens who react intelligently to the life about them, we must teach children to analyze the subject matter with which they deal,

*to discriminate between important and minor parts, to trace causal
relations, to estimate ethical values, to question the validity
of statements, to suspend judgment until data have been
accumulated sufficient to justify generalization."*

—*Bessie W. Stillman*

*"Everyone is born a genius,
but the process of living de-geniuses them."*

—*Buckminster Fuller*

O ne thing will solve America's public school problems.
Everything else will fail. If you are the administrator of a
school—public or private, or even home—at any level from kindergarten through graduate schools, you need to understand this
one thing. If you do, and if you take appropriate action, you will
succeed—your school will educate. If you don't, the school will
fail to achieve its potential to educate.

Since the famous *Nation at Risk* report in April of 1983, almost
everybody has been trying to "fix" American education, including
educators, policy-makers, parents, a string of U.S. Presidents, and
the courts. Eventually, since nobody else could seem to make
real changes, corporations, foundations and individual philanthropists poured billions into the cause. The result? Despite a few
limited victories, on the whole American education has gotten
consistently worse. Only 29% of U.S. fourth graders are proficient
readers,[30] and the U.S. is still 15th in reading, 14th in science and
18th in math among industrialized nations, and even lower if
non-industrialized nations are included.[31]

The one thing which has flourished in American education
since 1983 is the debate itself. Harvard professors, child psychol-
ogists and education researchers made a mint sharing their views,
and non-traditional educational lobbyists and gurus proliferated.
The content of their predictions and recommendations is mixed
and contradictory.

The Recent History of Educational Reform

In the 1980s the debate revolved around reforming public schools, including such proposals as increased teacher salaries, better training, increased funding, higher standards, upgraded technology in schools, better and wider testing, teacher training, etc. Even the direct testing of teachers was suggested. Some recommended a focus on the elementary grades, still others on high schools, and Allan Bloom's bestselling *The Closing of the American Mind* promoted the change in higher education, our colleges and universities (who do, after all, train the teachers, administrators and education experts). But Dewey had already answered this question, and Adler after him, by pointing out that regardless of how we think it *should* be, most college age students are naturally going to be focused on job training rather than education, so we'd better educate them before they turn eighteen.

Others suggested that we focus on improving pre-schools, since we can't fix all schools at once but it is certainly reasonable to revamp pre-school first and then just improve one year at a time. Ironically, this relatively quick fix of 15-20 years was rejected at least partially because we wanted things to improve sooner.

Of all these proposals during the eighties, many specific plans were drafted, analyzed and applied with differing, but generally low, impact. Quality education continued its path toward seeming extinction.

In the 1990s the debate turned to non-traditional educational models—charter schools, vouchers, corporate-run inner-city public schools, private schools, homeschooling, virtual online programs, and private scholarships. Authors like John Taylor Gatto, John Holt and Samuel Blumenfeld became popular in non-traditional education circles. Futurists such as Toffler, Naisbitt and techies like Bill Gates and Steve Jobs implied that virtual education, one-on-one computer to student, was the key. The result of these new ideas and options was positive. A freer market, it turns out, really does improve education—for those who take advantage of it. But the overwhelming majority of students in the

United States are still not getting a quality education. And, ironically, it tends to be just those segments of the population whose only real option is the public schools that are still stuck in a worsening downward spiral. Apparently the best we have to offer *them* is a rash of best-selling works by psychology professors—from Howard Gardner to Mel Levine—clarifying how a child's mind "really" works.

The Outcome of Educational Reform

Yet American education remains mediocre at best. Experts, philanthropists, legislators, lobbyists and especially parents grow weary of the seemingly endless, and fruitless, battle to improve American education. Each new fad breaks into state capitols, school boards and neighborhoods full of promise, only to fall flat like the last one. Each new political campaign promises to "really" fix education this time, but in the end students graduate and move on in an increasingly frustrating educational environment. The latest proposals from another "Education President" of No Child Left Behind are as hollow as similar Goals 2000, Outcome-Based Education, and Clinton educational "mandates."

Don't get me wrong: both liberal and conservative intentions are real, and massive resources have been and will continue to be put to work. For example, one report showed that "U.S. taxpayers spent an average of $107,000 to produce a proficient fourth grade reader…[from a low of $70,900 in the state of Utah to $172,000 in Hawaii and a whopping $420,000 in the District of Columbia], with about 29% of fourth graders at proficient level."[32] But these good intentions are hollow promises and the expenditures ineffective investments because they are based on two myths which have been part of American Education since about the turn of the last century. The current promises will fail as did the past efforts, and so will future reforms, until the myths are addressed.

Once the myths are clearly understood and rejected, then we must turn to solutions. The truth is that the solutions have been obvious all along: the children of the wealthy have been getting quality education all along, even since *A Nation at Risk* was published, and through all the debates of the 1980s, 1990s, and 2000s. How to provide quality education is clear, with only two obstacles: getting rid of the myths, and making the choice to change. The United States already has the ability and resources to do it—in financial terms, it likely won't cost more than we are already pouring into education. Yet it will achieve results.

But it will not be a quick fix. It is neglected now because it is *hard*. It is especially hard for our generation, because few of our educators, legislators or parents experienced a quality educational environment themselves. It hurts to admit that, but we must begin with the truth if we want real results. If you are one of these educators, such an admission directly impacts your profession and livelihood. But the question remains, how can a poorly educated (albeit highly trained) nation even begin to talk about fixing American education?

The answer is simple, but first we need to expose the misconceptions that short-circuit so many well-meaning, well-funded and truly committed attempts to redeem our failing public education system.

The Two Myths

The first myth, the fundamental root cause of American educational failure (as mentioned in Chapter Two), *is that it is possible for one human being to educate another*. It isn't. Every human being learns exactly as much as he or she chooses to learn. No more, no less. No exceptions. We can increase opportunity, incentive, motivation, and improve the environment, the materials, and the resources—but ultimately students must choose to learn or they won't. Where students consistently study hard, education improves.

The second myth is that the job of teachers is to educate. That isn't their role at all, not if they're effective. The role of teachers is to inspire. As previously stated, a teacher can't educate anyone but herself. A teacher can, however, inspire others—which is in fact the essence of teaching. Those who inspire, teach; those who don't...don't.

The inspiration is a combination of the teacher's example, hard work, and having the freedom by law and administration to pursue excellence in the art of teaching.

This is why I insist that the only person who can fix education is the student. The more popular options—increased funding, bigger schools, vouchers, the latest curriculum fad, the proliferation of private or charter schools, more homeschooling, and even well-intentioned federal acts—will not and can not fix American *education*. They may improve it, perhaps even significantly, but only to the extent that the individual student determines to educate self and then follows through. But few students study until they are inspired.

Teaching, not education, must be our focus, because great teaching inspires students to educate *themselves*. Great teaching will solve our educational problems—in public, charter, private, home, higher, and non-traditional schools. Find a great teacher, in any setting, and you will find a group of students diligently, enthusiastically and effectively educating themselves—in at-risk, inner-city public classrooms as well as elite, private prep schools.

In my experience, there is not a grave shortage of passionate individuals in the teaching profession (and indeed who enter the profession, year after year) with the drive, idealism and vision to make a difference in their students' lives. So, why is our public school system limping along with such universally poor output? The answer: Because we typically put teachers last.

Putting Teachers First

What I call "putting teachers first" is desperately needed in our schools. As I visit classrooms in public and private schools in the United States, two things seem to always stand out—the high quality of individuals in the teaching profession and the poor quality of overall education. It's hardly a secret: there are great teachers in practically every school in the United States. I have seen them in every single one of the dozens of schools I've visited. I make a point of searching them out. But hardly any of them are really doing it the way they could. They work within the system of policy and administration most of the time, saving their passion, genius and the risk of being inspiring for the few students who strike a chord with them. If you aren't one of these students, you get an uninspiring and mediocre education at best. This shocking dichotomy is the central challenge of modern education. Fix it, and we will fix American education. We must put teachers first.

If this sounds simplistic, consider the evidence. Find a model of great education in history and you will find a great teacher who inspired students to make the hard choice to study. Wherever you find such a teacher, you will also find self-motivated students who study hard. When students study hard, learning occurs.

Despite the current problems of education, I have seen much hope in the faces of thousands of teachers and parents I have spoken with across the nation. These dedicated teachers nearly all have in common a love for youth, demonstrated courage, and amazing energy and tenacity. But the system needs to get out of their way. They need to be given the tools and support to really teach.

American education must put teachers first. The goal or end result we all want is high-quality education. Of course, there are as many ideas about what that means as there are professional educators. But one thing is absolutely certain—we will never have high-quality education until students study hard, really hard, day in and day out. Let me be absolutely clear about this: When students don't study, no funding, program, policy, law, philanthropic donation, presidential mandate or anything else will provide quality education. When students freely and voluntarily choose to study hard, education improves. Over time it achieves excellence.

My second point is equally vital: To the extent they are hindered by policy and administration, teachers can't inspire students to want to study.

Finally, and just as essential: For over a hundred years, and especially in the last four decades, America's educational systems have consistently moved from supporting great teachers to making them practically powerless factory workers. The conveyer belt model of education has damaged student learning, yes, but it has almost destroyed great teaching. Without inspiring teachers, little study occurs. When this trend reverses, American education will improve.

We know this instinctively. Our whole society applauds it in movies like *Dead Poet's Society, Stand and Deliver, The School of Rock, Finding Forrester, Music of the Heart, Mr. Holland's Opus, Coach Carter*, and *The Emperor's Club*, to name just a few. Perhaps even more telling, consider how we respond to the *other* teachers in these movies, the uninspiring teachers and administrators who are trying to…well, educate, or run a school. Each of these popular movies shows us a great teacher inspiring students to study—pitted against peers, policy and administration which think teachers should educate. If even Hollywood understands this model, and if popular culture resonates with it so readily and virtually universally, *if this is such a self-evident truth*, what can be the justification for not putting the model into practice?

"DO IT"

At the risk of being redundant, let me reiterate: the solution to America's educational dilemma is to get students to voluntarily and passionately study hard, hours and hours, week after week, because it is what they *choose*. The only way to get such students is to give great teachers the freedom to excel, to inspire. We must put teachers first. The only way to put teachers first is to put them in charge—not of the schools, but of their classrooms.

The result of putting teachers first will be challenging and difficult. At least during the transitional period, putting teachers first will create chaos in the well-entrenched educational bureaucracy along with administrative and legislative nightmares. These are burdens we must bear or risk another generation of failure; weighing the one outcome against the other leaves us with little choice. It is worth it because it will create a nation of teachers who inspire and students who study. Education will finally be on the road to excellence.

This suggestion will not go over well with some administrators and legislators, perhaps not even with all businessmen and philanthropists—but what do they know about education? There is a long tradition of making fun of teachers who try to tell their students how to get rich; should we not question the moral authority of businessmen, politicians or administrators who propose to counsel us on teaching and education? Every U.S. Presidential Administration since 1983 has tried to get quality back into education, including the current one. Their goals and intentions are good, but they consistently add more policy and administrative restraints to great teachers. This only makes the problem worse. Until teachers are free to teach, they won't inspire; until teachers inspire, students won't love learning and study hard.

"But students just won't do that," the critics say. Of course they won't, until they're inspired. The inspired students *do* study hard—inspired students always do. The irony is that the schools already have inspiring teachers who simply aren't allowed to inspire. The myths must be faced head on and teachers must be given back their classrooms. When the handcuffs are taken off, teachers will inspire and students will study—and American public education will finally be on track to accomplish all that it can. America must put teachers first.

In the end, this is a call to courage and leadership to those who lead our public schools. May they define and fulfill their roles as the defenders of the classroom environment, and the teachers as the stewards of it.

CHAPTER EIGHT

Thomas Jefferson Education at College

"A university is…an Alma Mater, knowing her children one by one, not a factory, or a mint, or a treadmill."

—John Henry Newman

"It is easy to see that the moral sense has been bred out of certain sections of the population, like the wings have been bred off certain chickens to produce more white meat on them. This is a generation of wingless chickens…."

—Flannery O'Connor

"The actual teaching is…selected and controlled…by the business interests playing on the vested academic interests."

—J.A. Hobson, 1909

"Compared with the medieval university, the contemporary university has developed the mere seed of professional instruction into an enormous activity; it has added the function of research; and it has abandoned almost entirely the teaching or transmission of culture."

—Jose Ortega y Gasset[33]

In 1636 Harvard was founded, starting the Founding phase of American education. It was followed by Yale in 1701, Princeton in 1746, and William and Mary, Columbia, Brown, Rutgers and Dartmouth, among others, by 1769. These schools trained the Founding Fathers, who established this nation's Constitution and safeguarded its freedoms.

How did they do it? In the decades leading up to the Revolutionary War, the average college had several dozen students and a few faculty members. Schools of over a hundred students were uncommon. Students read the Bible and classics; prepared textbooks were rare. Lectures were limited to special occasions, and nearly all studies centered around a table with a teacher and a few students discussing what they had read. Many teachers used simulations to get students involved. In fact, George Wythe was the first teacher in the Colonies to use moot courts and mock congresses.

This great system of education, though in decline by the 1850s, lingered in a few places as late as the 1880s. As student Frederic Howe wrote of his experience at Johns Hopkins: the students and even faculty "were badly housed in a group of old lofts and residences on Howard Street. There were no fraternities, playing fields or organized sports. Instead of the conventional rows of chairs with passive students facing a professor, the teacher and his students sat in...old chairs around a long table. Teachers and students alike felt a dignity and enthusiasm in their work," and we "wondered at the intimacy between professors and students."[34]

Four Trends Away from The Founding Colleges

The second phase in the history of American colleges started in the 1850s and continues today. It is characterized by four major trends. First, the move from religious to secular. All the Ivy League schools were founded by churches with the goal of training leaders who loved God and understood the Bible, but God was slowly edited out of the curriculum and eventually prohibited in many schools.

The second trend was the replacement of leadership education with job training. Today it is difficult to find a person who thinks schools have any other purpose than job training, much less an emphasis on classical leadership studies in the liberal arts.

The third trend away from our Founding colleges had to do with the curriculum. Reading and discussing classics, which taught students how to think, was replaced with prepared text-books and lectures designed to teach students what to think, and a grading system to enforce it. The new "conveyor belt" system was even thrust upon faculty through tenure.

The fourth trend can be summed up as "bigger is better." For example, in the decade between 1890 and 1900, the number of college teachers in the U.S. doubled, though the number of students did not. But as schools hired more and more teachers over the next century, classroom sizes got bigger and bigger. Many schools stopped measuring themselves according to quality and began defining themselves by quantity.

Robert Hutchins, President of the University of Chicago, put it this way: "Under this system the intellectual progress of the young is determined by the time they have been in attendance, the number of hours they have sat in classes, and the proportion of what they have been told that they can repeat on examinations. Undoubtedly, fine associations, fine buildings, green grass, good food, and exercise are excellent things for anybody. You will note that they are exactly what is advertised by every resort hotel. The reason that they are also advertised by every college and university is that we have no coherent educational program to announce."[35]

Even today's community colleges are many times larger than the small schools which prepared the Founding generation, and the output of both systems provides convincing evidence that theirs was superior. Our country began with a college system that produced the likes of Jefferson, Madison and Webster; then we turned to a system which dismissed God, the classics, and the proven methods of the centuries. It wasn't long before people began noticing the decline. A popular song of the era went like this:

We sing in praise of college
of MA's and Ph.D's
But in pursuit of knowledge
We are starving by degrees

Although we have made great gains in technical and specialized training in this second phase, and great strides in including
women and minorities, clearly we have declined in morality,
leadership and quality.

Back to the Future

Today we are seeing the birth of a third phase of American college education, a return to the foundations of classics/mentors
education. Colleges such as St. John's, Thomas Aquinas, Thomas
More and a few others seem to signal a move in the right direction. George Wythe College has attempted to go all the way back
to the Founding system. We focus on small over big, classics
over textbooks, discussion and mentoring over lecture, leadership over job training, and—above all—God over secular. We are
not specifically denominational, but neither are we secular in the
modern sense of "no faith allowed." The expression and sharing
of each student's religious views and beliefs is encouraged. Our
goal is to help create a new generation of statesmen like that of the
Founding Fathers and Mothers—entrepreneurs and statesmen
who will leaven society and elevate the world.

With all this said, I would like to extend a caution to the
young person who is considering college and to the student who
is nearing graduation or has graduated from college. As potential
leaders, three great challenges loom ahead.

Warning One: Pride

The first is pride: *your* pride. You have worked hard to be where
you are, and many will honor you as you increase your knowledge, talents and achievements. You must not take these honors
too seriously; most importantly, you must not let them unduly

influence your decisions. After you weigh the pros and cons, choose to attend the *right* college, the one most likely to help you attain a world-class education and prepare you for your mission, purpose and goals in life. Choose the right school, the right job, the right opportunities, not just the most prestigious.

Likewise, there are many who are less fortunate than you, less educated, perhaps less talented. Never look down on them. Serve them. This is a great key to life: lose your life in service and you will become great. Do what is right, even when it is difficult, *especially* when it is difficult. Do not make the mistake of being a social climber. Of course you will want to use your knowledge and skills and talents to do great things, but do them because they are right, because they are good, not because they make you look good.

There may also be those who discount or undermine your attempts to improve the world, who laugh at your educational or career choices. Let them. And while you let them, quietly set out to serve them. You are not changing the world in order to impress them, you are doing it because it is right. The classics taught you this. Live up to it.

Warning Two: Superficiality

The second challenge you must overcome is superficiality. The world teaches that good grades equal intelligence, but they don't; that degrees are equal to education, but they aren't; that money and position are success, but they aren't.

Do not buy the facades the world offers. Only virtue is success. Only integrity is greatness. Your task is to become "men and women of virtue, wisdom, diplomacy and courage who inspire greatness in others and move the cause of liberty,"[36] to live up to your mentors and the classics which helped make you who you are and will help build the person you will become.

Warning Three: The Mundane

The third challenge you will face is the challenge of the mundane. As a student or an employee, you may not always be invigorated by your work. As a resident of a small town, or lost in a big city, you may long for the excitement of "greener pastures." As a freshman, or father and husband, you may long for the limelight of career, financial or social position. As a roommate, or wife and mother, some of you will face a seemingly never-ending pile of laundry, dishes and housework. You may wonder what happened to the "great expectations" of leadership abilities that you learned in the classics.

Yet it is in exactly such circumstances that the character of leaders, statesmen, Founding Fathers and Mothers is forged. It is in the small and simple things that greatness is obtained. When the day comes that you are called upon for what the *world* calls "great things," you will see clearly that they are no greater than the things you did at home.

By the way, that call *will* come. If you have paid the price of greatness through classics and mentors, and if you continue to pay the price of greatness in the next phase of your education— the everyday-life phase—you will become great, and you will be called upon to change the world.

Searching Out a College

There are many colleges that follow the classics/mentors model; seek them out, prepare for them, and pay the price required to get a superb education. Or, if you are counseling children in the matter, help them do the same.

The exception is where your goals and direction require extensive professional training; even here, professional programs should only be entered in most cases *after* you have obtained a solid liberal arts education.

Most schools offer advanced placement or concurrent enrollment courses with colleges, and it is now possible for most homeschoolers to complete homeschool by fifteen or sixteen, complete a strong classics/mentors college program partly through distance studies and then on campus, and still go to professional programs at ages eighteen or nineteen when most American students enter college. It has been my experience that the on-campus experience is vital, for a minimum of two years, mainly for the interaction with world-class mentors and peers.

The leaders of the future will come from the schools, homes, colleges, universities and organizations where classics, mentors and the other elements of Thomas Jefferson Education are cherished and seriously pursued. If you are in a setting where they are not used, adopt them. It is never too late—if your own college experience did not center around the classics/mentors model, you should consider searching out a college or equivalent experience and getting to work on becoming a leader of the Twenty-first Century.

CHAPTER NINE

Leadership Careers

*"No, Mr. Regan. The United States will continue to be
a great manufacturing power.
There just won't be as high a percentage of people
working in factories."*

—Heidi Toffler

*"The basic economic resource…is no longer capital, nor natural
resources…nor labor. It is and will be knowledge.
The central wealth-creating activities will be neither the allocation
of capital to productive uses, nor labor.…The Leading social groups
of the knowledge society will be "knowledge workers"—
knowledge executives who know how to allocate knowledge
to productive use, just as the capitalists knew how to
allocate capital to productive use; knowledge professionals;
knowledge employees."*

—Peter Drucker

*"A career in business is not only a morally serious
vocation but a morally noble one.
Those who are called to it have reason to take pride
in it and rejoice in it."*

—Michael Novak

In the next thirty years, certain people will have successful careers and certain people will not. The most important factor determining which type of career you will have is education. Notice that I didn't say "diploma" or "degree," but rather "education." Your education may literally determine your future. The public, professional and leadership systems train you for very different things.

The economy is changing and many so-called experts are saying things like, "In fifteen years, there will be these kinds of jobs; in twenty years there will be those kinds of jobs." There's enough variance among opinions that we don't really have an exact picture, but there is enough similarity in the predictions that we can get a few general ideas. Based on historical and current trends, it appears that:

The conveyor belt educated will tend to spend their working years in moderate to low-income production, service and government jobs.

Professional school graduates will naturally tend to be in management and the professions, but there will be fewer jobs in these fields in the coming years and those that remain will be less prosperous. Mid-level management is being downsized and the professions are changing from the independent, lucrative fields they once were to managed, institutionalized, bureaucratic systems with fewer financial or social rewards.

Of course, production, service, government, management and professional fields all need leadership, and this will tend to be supplied by those who have learned how to think: analysts, entrepreneurs, decision makers, statesmen.[37]

Success in any field requires training—formal or informal—in the central principles which govern it. How many successful attorneys are there who never went to law school? Or dentists who never studied dentistry? Or entrepreneurs who never learned the principles of entrepreneurship? Or successful statesmen who never learned statesmanship? The principles of successful leadership, entrepreneurship and statesmanship are the lessons taught in a leadership education system, from classics and mentors, and of course from the practical application and experience which good mentors always demand.

Some of you may be thinking: "My Mary is just not a leader. She is a good girl, yes, but not a leader." Don't give in to that mindset. It comes from our public socialization and the false idea that a leader is someone with smooth charisma and a TV personality. This is false. Jefferson hated to speak in public and hardly ever did. Madison was sickly, shy and quiet. John Adams was considered abrasive and annoying. Lincoln was homely and lost many more elections than he won. Columbus couldn't convince anyone for years and years. Joan of Arc was from a poor family in a little farm community. Leadership isn't something that just happens to you; it is a choice, a choice to pay the price to be great. It isn't a certain set of talents, but rather a choice to develop your *own* talents, to use classics, mentors, hard work and faith to *become* great. Of course your Mary, your Bobby, your Kimberly are not leaders yet; they haven't earned it. But they can. You can if you will pay the price.

Your Career Plan

Considering the three systems of education (conveyor belt, professional, leadership) and the careers they prepare you for (low income, professional, decision maker), which one do you want to emphasize? Which one do you want for your children? If you want to be in low-income, production, service, government jobs, you ought to be in a conveyor belt school; because that's what it will prepare you for, and it will do it effectively. The whole nation benefits when schools are available for all and there is a general level of literacy and job preparation.

But if you want more, you'd better get into another system. Of course, people can use one system to move to another; if you do well enough in a public school, you can get scholarships and other opportunities in the professional system. But if you want to get leadership education, you will need to find a mentor and get into the classics. The impact of this decision on your career and future is tremendous.

It is important to realize that an individual with a leadership education may choose whatever vocation he or she pleases, be it "blue collar," "service," "management," "professional," or "entrepreneur," etc. But with his or her leadership education, the vocation is not a dead-end without prerogatives. It is a venue of service that suits the leader's interests, talents and timing. Any time such an individual chooses to reinvent his career choice, he has the skills and vision to do so. But this is only true if he has the education and preparation that afford him that freedom.

The best place to start is to find a mentor. For the very young, the best mentor is likely a parent. Then somewhere around ages 12-15, you and your children together start looking for additional mentors to take you further. When it comes time for college or even a professional school (*after* they have a great leadership education), help them find schools where classics and mentors are emphasized.

Education is the start of a successful career, but, ironically, students who focus on career preparation instead of getting a great education are unlikely to achieve the success they desire. A superb education is the first key, and must be pursued with an eye toward gaining both knowledge and skills.

Harvard Skills

For your children to really learn how to think and to become leader-statesmen, they need to master several essential skills. The first list comes from Harvard School of Law, and includes ten things deemed necessary for success in the job market of the Twenty-first Century:[38]

1. The ability to define problems without a guide.

When was the last time you saw that rewarded in a school setting? Picture it: the teacher hands out a history exam. Johnny raises his hand and says, "There's a problem with the question. You assume in the question that Napoleon was motivated by—"

"Be quiet, Johnny, you're interrupting again. And by the way, I'm timing you all."

The ability to *define* problems without a guide—now that's leadership. Not just to solve problems; it doesn't take a great genius to solve most problems once they are clearly and accurately defined. The tendency in all three systems of education is to teach: "Solve the problem." But in leadership education you teach students to clearly define it; only then do they work on solutions. Once they really know the problem inside-out, the solution is often simple. One basic math textbook I highly recommend, *Applied Mathematics* by Glenn and Julianne Kimber, teaches the math principle and has the student write the problems; then they solve them. Saxon math texts also require self-guided student work and thinking. This is the classics approach—teach the principle, and then have the student apply it.

2. *The ability to ask hard questions which challenge prevailing assumptions.*

Can you imagine that being rewarded in a math class? The geometry teacher declares, "This right angle is—"

"Ms. Smith," Johnny interrupts, "you're basing this all on Euclid's Theorem and, in fact, Gauss and other thinkers through Einstein showed that Euclidean geometry was very limited in actual application."

"What are you talking about? This is how you do the problem in this class if you don't want to fail."

Hopefully, as parents and teachers, this isn't our methodology. If you are going to train him to be a leader, then tell Johnny, "That's a great thought, son. Now prove it to me mathematically. Or write and present a paper expounding that idea." Then follow up on it. The student leads; the mentor guides, questions, counsels.

3. *The ability to quickly assimilate needed data from masses of irrelevant information.*

This is absolutely essential in the Information Age. We are inundated with information, but most of it does us very little good. Only the relevant, important information is of value; it takes *thinking* to separate the important from the rest. Most textbooks are among the worst places to learn relevance, since most of them seem committed to spouting reams of disconnected data as discussed in C.S. Lewis' *The Abolition of Man*. The classics, on the other hand, are the seedbed of the important, the relevant, the enduring.

4. *The ability to work in teams without guidance.*

There are five of you; no appointed leader; no structure; with a major problem to solve. What do you do? How do you get the group to cooperate? How do you make the best use of everyone's ideas, talents and skills? First, define the problem. Second, coalesce the team. Third, incentivize creativity. Fourth, decide together. Fifth, make an action plan based on integrity and volunteerism. Sixth, synergize and achieve. Seventh, evaluate and improve. Eighth, define the next problem.

The order changes based on what the problem is, so you have to experience this. Books aren't enough. Teachers can do wonders with project learning—every classroom should have at least one such project going all the time.

Note that homeschool is great for these activities; homeschools may not provide the racial and cultural diversity of public schools, but they can remedy this by including neighbors and other homeschoolers. They do have one thing public classrooms almost never have: age diversity, which is much closer to real-life situations than segregated age groups. Put your students in these situations—vicariously through the classics, in planned scenarios you create, and in real life situations such as work, a family business, a political campaign or local cause. Then openly discuss lessons learned, mistakes and their correctives, ideas for future action, etc.

5. *The ability to work absolutely alone.*

Not just quietly, but actually alone, with nobody to help. This means giving the students responsibility instead of just tasks.

Students need to learn to direct their own education, always with feedback from the mentor, and to analyze the level of quality, and rework it until it is truly excellent. The mentor ensures that there is open discussion and honest feedback afterwards in order to increase the learning, retention, and application of lessons learned.

6. *The ability to persuade others that your course is the right one.*

Communication, written and spoken, is essential to leadership. These skills come from reading great writing and listening to great speaking, then critiquing and discussing it, and finally practicing it. Mentor and coach: the student writes, you critique it together, and he rewrites—over and over and over until it is high-quality work.

In addition to technique, persuasion comes from confidence and passion. People are not forced or constrained to become leaders; they are nurtured, loved, led and guided. The passion comes from a conviction of what is right.

7. *The ability to conceptualize and reorganize information into new patterns.*

Leaders learn from the past and have a vision of the future, but they live in the present. So students must learn to see how information fits, how it can be reshaped in a given situation, how it can be used to answer questions and influence outcomes. Connection is the key to leadership, and where most schools tend to separate academic subjects and focus on specialization, great teachers, "Jefferson Teachers," correlate subjects and help students become specialists in thinking, communicating and leading.

8. *The ability to discuss ideas with an eye toward application.*

Leaders don't just memorize, they apply. They *do* things. Knowledge is only as powerful as its result, as how the students use it to make a difference in the world. Each time the student reads a classic, writes a paper, does an assignment of any kind, the mentor should initiate a discussion on the application of the lessons learned, of how the student can use this information to deal with real-life concerns and current issues. Over time this creates a habit of thinking in terms of solutions. The fact is that there are answers to nearly all problems, and leadership consists of matching up the answers with the problems and inspiring others to do likewise.

9 & 10. The ability to think inductively, deductively and dialectically.

Students must learn to draw specific conclusions based on a wide body of evidence, and also to induce and project, based on minimal data or minor trends. Both scholarly precision and trust of intuition are essential to effective leadership. Students must also learn to fully explore both sides of a debate in order to arrive at truth, and then to see all the other sides of the same argument, including the possible results of every potential decision.

Princeton Skills

In 1993, a committee at Princeton University outlined similar skills, their list of goals for undergraduate education, which are interesting for comparison and add several new ideas:

- The ability to think, speak, and write clearly.
- The ability to reason critically and systematically.
- The ability to conceptualize and solve problems.
- The ability to think independently.
- The ability to take initiative and work independently.
- The ability to work in cooperation with others and learn collaboratively.
- The ability to judge what it means to understand something thoroughly.
- The ability to distinguish the important from the trivial, the enduring from the ephemeral.
- Familiarity with different modes of thought (including quantitative, historical, scientific, and aesthetic).
- Depth of knowledge in a particular field.

- The ability to see connections among disciplines, ideas and cultures.
- The ability to pursue life-long learning.[39]

Wythe Skills

At George Wythe College, a group of students and faculty looked over the Harvard and Princeton lists and determined that while such skills might earn you good grades in school and success in a career, they won't win you happiness. We then provided the following list of items which should be part of an education and are essential preparation for success in the future:

- The ability to understand human nature and lead accordingly.
- The ability to identify needed personal traits and turn them into habits.
- The ability to establish, maintain and improve lasting relationships.
- The ability to keep one's life in proper balance.
- The ability to discern truth and error regardless of the source, or the delivery.
- The ability to discern *true* from *right*.
- The ability and discipline to do right.
- The ability and discipline to constantly improve.

By finding ways to teach these thirty skills (and perhaps others which you and your students think of), and helping students master them, you will be building yourself into a Jefferson Teacher and your students into leaders, analysts, entrepreneurs and statesmen.

Mentors, Classics and Career Success

The best careers of the future require the ability to think and the skills to lead. While technical and professional training is essential, it is the students with both technical/professional *and* leadership education who will excel. As one graduate student wrote: "Students may well ask how a liberal arts education can help them in the job market. There are real usable skills that are imparted in a classical education. In fact, they are the *most* usable skills colleges can give. Billy W. Wireman, President of Queens College has said, 'Let us recall that the language of arts, those abilities to speak and act thoughtfully and coherently, first evolved, in ancient times, not as academic specialties, but as practical tools of the citizen. The liberal arts are designed not as aides in speculation, but as means for action.' The liberal arts are the arts of communication and thinking. 'They are the arts indispensable to further learning, for they are the arts of reading, writing, speaking, listening, figuring,' commented well-known educator Robert M. Hutchins. These are the skills which are helping liberal arts graduates get jobs, really *good* jobs: in many fields the best jobs, the leadership jobs. More and more companies, even specialized ones, are willing to spend lots of money on training if they can just find bright employees with strong communication, analytical, and interpersonal skills.

"The liberal arts are even useful in Silicon Valley. 'The modern world lives by the products of technology. Technology, in turn, depends on human ingenuity; high technology depends on highly trained ingenuity. If, however, expertise is to be transformed into creative ingenuity, what is required is a broader perspective and an elasticity of mind that technology training alone cannot provide,' reports Professor Moulakis of the University of Colorado— Boulder.

"When corporations want students with excellent writing skills, analytical and problem-solving skills, organizational skills, good interpersonal relations skills, they look for liberal arts majors. David Reed, director of Andersen Consulting, based in Chicago, says, 'We look for people who are smart. We look for someone who is a critical thinker, someone who examines the pros and cons of a decision before deciding....'

"Many companies actually seek out liberal arts graduates. According to Nick Burkholder, Assistant Vice President of

Corporate Staffing for Cinga Corporation, 'The liberal arts degree is the best degree for a career in business. [It] starts the process of thinking....' Liberal arts graduates are working in business, law, medicine, and technology. They are uniquely prepared to excel in any field because they have learned how to think, how to communicate and how to learn.

"Although 75% of parents and 85% of students still believe the point of college is to get a practical education and land a decent job right away, many CEO's are recommending long-term career development. According to a new study by Gobart and William Smith Colleges, in Geneva, N.Y., only 37% of the CEO's queried said that the purpose of a degree is to acquire work skills. Ninety percent of business leaders called the humanities essential to developing critical thinking and 77% said they are necessary for problem-solving skills. As far as the employability of liberal arts graduates, business has learned what schools should remember: that thinking comes before doing, because thought guides deeds....Corporate restructuring has placed an emphasis on efficiency and those who can do more than one job...."

"It is commonly said that the liberal arts will earn you less than more technical degrees, but according to Ramon Greenwood, former senior vice-president of American Express and job-hunting expert, 'People who write well and market themselves with flair will be snapped up faster than a computer nerd with no communication skills. Show them some street smarts as well as that degree. Show them you know how to operate in the real world.' And finally, from Jones, 'I've got news for you: People don't hire degrees, they hire people.'"[40]

The leadership education of Thomas Jefferson, Benjamin Franklin, James Madison, George Washington, and the Founding generation helped make America great. As changes and challenges come in the Twenty-first Century, somewhere there must be those who are prepared to step forward and lead. Since leaders in history are trained by mentors and classics, homes and schools that apply the principles of a Thomas Jefferson Education are crucially needed to nurture, train and prepare many of these much needed leaders, entrepreneurs and statesmen of the Twenty-first Century.

But this will only occur if educators—home, public and private—put the conveyor belt behind them and turn to classics and mentoring.

CHAPTER TEN

Statesmanship: Making a Difference in Society

*"What the statesman is most anxious to produce
is a certain moral character in his fellow citizens,
namely a disposition to virtue and the
performance of virtuous acts."*

—*Aristotle*

*"He that is a righteous master of his house
will be a righteous statesman."*

—*Plato*

"You must be the change you wish to see in the world."

—*Ghandi*

I n 1764 Thomas Jefferson was just a twenty-one-year-old college student. He had just been "dumped" by his intended, who married one of his best friends. Worse still, Jefferson was asked to serve as the best man at the wedding. With no other romantic prospects, he focused on his studies under his mentor, George Wythe.

In that same year, George Washington was just a farmer. He worked hard trying to make a living, and one of his major efforts that year was a struggle to get out of debt.

John Adams was a teacher for a small community school. He courted and married Abigail in October of that same year, 1764.

In 1764 James Madison turned twelve years old, and his future wife hadn't even been born yet. He was a good student but known as "quiet" and "shy."

A decade later these men and their peers would courageously declare independence from the greatest power in the world and sign it, "we...pledge our lives, our fortunes, and our sacred honor."

A decade after that they would write the *Constitution of the United States*, "the most wonderful work ever struck off at a given time by the brain and purpose of man," as Gladstone put it.[41]

But in 1764 they were just ordinary people, like you and me. In fact, they were a lot like you and me.

It is not enough to reverence the Founding Fathers each year at the Fourth of July, or even other times.

We must be like them.

Their writings show that they knew the cycles of history. Jefferson wrote: "History, by apprising the people of the past, will enable them to judge the future..."[42] Alexander Tytler, also writing in the Founding era, said: "...the world's greatest civilizations...have progressed through this sequence: from bondage to spiritual faith; from spiritual faith to great courage; from courage to liberty; from liberty to abundance; from abundance to selfishness; from selfishness to complacency; from complacency to apathy; from apathy to dependency; from dependency back again to bondage."[43]

Knowing this pattern of history, the Founders knew that courageous and wise statesmen would be needed shortly. They could not see the future, but it was clear to them that crisis was coming, and so they prepared.

Do the patterns of their day apply today? Might there be a future Jefferson, Madison, or Washington reading this book?

I believe that when the time is right, some of you will be called upon to be the statesmen of our day—whether you like it or not. And whether you are prepared or not.

What is a Statesman?

But what, exactly, is a statesman? Historically the term "statesmen" has been used to emphasize governmental leaders of the highest caliber, such as Washington, Lincoln, Churchill and Ghandi. But true statesmen are leaders in more than government; indeed they lead society as a whole. In our day, the character traits of statesmanship are needed in all areas of society.

As Shawn Ercanbrack wrote, a statesman is a "certain type of leader, one who takes character and moral courage into small business and major corporations, the media and entertainment, homes and families, schools and universities, hospitals and law firms, the military or the clergy, and government.…[Statesmen] apply statesmanship to industry, academia, government or whatever career path they choose. Individuals with such training think and act in a certain way. Their decisions are rooted in history, based on true principles and made concerning the long-term impact on society. The result is an uncommon individual, guided by virtue, wisdom, diplomacy and courage."

Virtue. Two types of virtue are essential to statesmanship: *private virtue*, which consists of basic honesty, integrity and character, in both public trusts and in one's personal life; and *public virtue*, voluntarily sacrificing personal comfort or benefits for the good of the nation or community. Virtue is listed as the first of the four character traits, as all true greatness flows from goodness, core integrity, and the willingness to sacrifice and serve. As Albert Schweitzer put it: "I don't know what your destiny will be, but one thing I know: the only ones among you who will really be happy are those who have sought and found how to serve."

Wisdom. The wise statesman has mastered the ability to seek and obtain effective answers to problems, to foresee the ramifications of potential actions and to implement solutions by the most enlightened means available. Alfred North Whitehead said, "The habits of the active utilization of well-understood principles is the final possession of wisdom." Wisdom combines knowledge, understanding and the ability to apply them effectively.

Diplomacy. Good ideas, however ideal, must be applied in the real world by real people in order to make a positive difference. Statesmen must build bridges, build on common ground, find and implement alternatives and cooperate with others to accomplish the most important goals.

Courage. Adversity and challenge are the terrain of statesmanship and only courage successfully carries the day. Winston Churchill said, "Courage is rightly esteemed the first of human qualities because it is the quality which guarantees all the others." Statesmen need courage both to act and to act *rightly*. Statesmen must exercise their will, choose to act and persevere. As Churchill also said, "Never, never, never give up." Courage is the catalyst of other character traits; it allows one to choose, act and endure.

The ability to inspire greatness in others. This is done by personifying greatness yourself, both by what you say and who you are. To inspire greatness is to model it for others, to communicate it effectively, and then to catalyze and lead action.

The ability to move the cause of liberty. Movement requires action. The cause of liberty is that of "life, liberty and the pursuit of happiness," where every man and woman is able to accept personal accountability and pursue happiness as they see fit within the bounds of proper behavior toward others. To move the cause of liberty, statesmen must combine the characteristics of virtue, wisdom, diplomacy, courage, and greatness.

The Need for Statesmen

There is a great need for statesmen in our day. Shawn Ercanbrack said: "There is a critical shortage of statesmen in the world. Schools in many nations are preparing students for specialty careers in service and industry, and training organizations provide additional instruction beyond the classroom. But where are the schools which specifically and effectively train statesmen: citizen-statesmen in the homes and communities? Entrepreneurs and statesmen in business? Or governmental statesmen to lead states and nations?"

Homeschools are ideal places to train statesmen, as are public and private schools and colleges which adopt the TJEd model. But educating statesmen presents unique challenges because both character and intellect must be taught. Statesmen must be inspired (by good teachers), trained (through emulation and coaching) and educated (through their own hard work).

If we are to become statesmen, how should you and I prepare? After all, we are just ordinary people.

How did the *ordinary* people in 1764 come to be the world's greatest statesmen in 1776 and 1787? They prepared the same way great statesmen have always prepared. And if we want to be as effective as they were, we must do as they did.

The great statesmen in history, each within their own circumstance, have used five keys on the path to greatness—at George Wythe College we call these The Five Pillars of Statesmanship:

Pillar One: Classics. Most great men and women of history studied other great men and women of history. Find a great statesman and you will find someone who studied the classics. Today there are many suggested lists, but for the Founders a classic was an original work by another great leader.

In a way, all great leaders have a line of authority back through the people they studied. Jefferson's heritage includes John Locke, the Anglo-Saxons and Jesus Christ. Madison's line follows Hume, Montesquieu, Aristotle and Moses. Lincoln's includes George Washington, Shakespeare and the Bible.

Some of these names may be unfamiliar—but that is exactly the point. Jefferson, Madison and Washington were not familiar with them until they read them, until they cracked the books. They weren't a different breed of men that we could never hope to emulate. They were people like you and me who paid the price to come face-to-face with greatness by experiencing the works of other great men and women and then applying what they learned. If we pay that same price, we can achieve the same results.

A person who comes face-to-face with Moses before Pharaoh, Socrates at the court in Athens, Paul on Mars Hill or before Agrippa, Thomas More in his own defense at Henry's court, Martin Luther's "Here I stand!" at the Diet of Wyrms, or Cromwell's decision to be King, is changed by the examples and experiences of those who have gone before.

How can there be Washingtons and Jeffersons today unless we read what they read, feel what they felt, and know what they knew? There are eternal principles upon which success in any field is based—and the way to find the principles of statesmanship is not in textbooks, but in the lives and writings of great statesmen.

Our freedoms are not the result of chance; we have them because the willing men and women of the Founding era chose to pay the price for freedom. Unless we are willing to pay that same price, we cannot and will not stay free.

Pillar Two: Mentors. The second pillar on the pathway to greatness is Mentors. Behind every Jefferson there is a George Wythe, behind every Madison a John Witherspoon, behind every Washington a Colonel Fairfax. These names are all but forgotten now, but they pushed their mentees to excellence, opened doors for their advancement, and gave them wise counsel throughout their lives.

Find a great man or woman and you will find a mentor or mentors inspiring and guiding them along their path.

Pillar Three: Simulations. Statesmen practice in order to prepare. Almost anything can be simulated: historical events, business concerns, current events, governmental situations, futuristic scenarios and so on. Simulations have a long tradition with broad application: from moot courts to mock parliament, role-plays to athletic scrimmages, military maneuvers to operations on cadavers. A key part of leadership education is simulating realistic scenarios in a non-threatening environment where coaching can help students prepare effectively for the real thing.

Pillar Four: Field Experience. Most great men and women in history had a variety of real-life experiences before they were called upon to exhibit greatness and leadership. Internships, employment, travel, participation in real events and other experiences can be very helpful to future statesmen—especially if done under the guiding hand of a seasoned and nurturing mentor and coach. Thomas Jefferson's life was changed by being present at Patrick Henry's moving speech, and Washington's role in the French and Indian War was vital preparation for the later mantle of leadership. If we are to become statesmen, we must get involved now in our communities and society. Future statesmen stand for something *now*.

Pillar Five: God. Great statesmen have experience with inspiration. Often these very public people keep their spiritual lives private, but their journals and papers acknowledge the hand of the Almighty. Whatever a person's religion or belief system, greatness requires a relationship with truth, inspiration, and absolutes.

Unknown Statesmen and Stateswomen

If Jefferson is right about the lessons of history, America will yet face challenges as grave as those the Founders faced. Who will be the statesmen that carry off freedom triumphant in *our* lifetime? When crises come, who will lead out? Where are the new American Founders of the Twenty-first Century?

None of us know who those statesmen will be. But this I do know—the great statesmen and stateswomen of the future will be prepared through The Five Pillars of Statesmanship.

The classics will probably not be handed to you on a silver platter. Nor is it likely that the perfect mentor will call you on the phone offering his or her services. You must seek these and the other pillars with energy and effort.

I know that it is hard to study the classics and find mentors.

We are busy making a living or going to school, but if we are too busy to study the classics and apply the lessons they teach, then we are too busy to stay free, too busy to secure the blessings of liberty to ourselves and our posterity.

Freedom is not an entitlement; it must be earned. It must be deserved.

By the way, some of the greatest statesmen in history are men and women you have never heard of. Being a statesman doesn't mean you are famous or even involved in government; it means that you demonstrate virtue, wisdom, diplomacy and courage in whatever you are called upon to do.

Become a Statesman

Statesmen are needed in our day, in our communities, homes, businesses, schools, churches, governments, relationships and associations.

In 1776 Thomas Jefferson declared the independence of all humankind, but in 1764 he was just a college student trying to mend a broken heart.

In 1780 George Washington almost single-handedly brought down the greatest military force on earth, but in 1764 he was just a farmer struggling to get out of debt.

In 1787 James Madison swayed the entire course of history, but in 1764 he was just a shy twelve-year-old.

It is the ordinary people in our day, just like those in 1764, who have greatness within them, *if they decide to develop it.*

They develop it through classics, mentors, simulations, field experience and a relationship with God. What would Jefferson have been without Locke, Washington without the experience of Cromwell, Madison without Montesquieu?

The Founders were great men and women of genius and inspiration, but it didn't just happen to them. They were ordinary people who chose to live good, honest lives and to pay the price of greatness.

In our day, the world cries out for good, honest people to pay that same price. Make your own education a Thomas Jefferson Education, then pass it on to your children, and begin exerting statesmanship in your community—and you will become the change you wish to see in the world

A New Golden Age?

"By three methods we may learn wisdom. First, by reflection, which is the noblest; second, by imitation, which is the easiest; and third, by experience, which is the bitterest."

—*Confucius*

During the sweltering summer of 1787, Benjamin Franklin wondered if the carved sun on the president's chair at the Constitutional Convention symbolized a rising sun or a setting sun. The success of the new nation confirmed that it represented America's rise. Two centuries later, a number of experts in many fields have expressed doubts about America's future and predicted American decline, including Allan Bloom, Paul Kennedy, Samuel Huntington, Robert Bork, Philip Bobbitt and Thomas Friedman, among others.

Will the Twenty-first Century be an American Epilogue, or a new Golden Age? This profound question has yet to be answered. It could go either way.

One thing is certain: Tomorrow's leaders will determine whether the flame of freedom and prosperity lit by American Founders two hundred years ago continues to burn brightly or is extinguished.

These leaders are being prepared today. Is their education up to par with their potential? For most of our youth, the answer is simply, "no." Parents, teachers, administrators, legislators and all of us are in a position to change this, and the time to start is now. My conviction is that the predictions of decline are overrated. I believe that the century which opened with the fall of two towers on September 11, 2001, will close with the American flag still waving proudly above many new towers across the United States. American industry and technology will be the best in the world and our society and economy will be the standard of freedom for the world. But this prediction depends on our choosing an education worthy of such a future. We simply must offer our children and grandchildren a high-quality leadership education.

Over fifteen years ago I went on a quest to find a great education. I studied (and in some cases visited or enrolled in) the great private and public university system, technical and professional schools, think tanks and corporate training programs, community and small colleges, unaccredited and non-traditional schools, distance and electronic studies, and every other educational offering I could find. I wondered why such a wealth of educational offerings did not seem to deliver greater educational results. What I discovered was surprisingly simple. Classics and mentors—the two components always present in truly great education—were neglected or had been entirely abandoned in most of America's educational settings. Restoring classics and mentors to American education will transform it. Nothing else will—not size, tradition, prestige, money, business acumen or technology.

My search for great education led me to help establish George Wythe College. Fourteen years ago, confronting serious first-year financial and founding challenges, I faced the dilemma of whether or not to keep this fledgling school open. I remember standing outside late one sleepless evening looking up at the stars. It was a clear night with no moon, but the stars were so bright that the front yard was entirely illuminated and I could see the mountains above the tree line. I remember thinking, "This is crazy! We have no savings. The college has no reserves, and not enough money to cover the bills we already have, much less have enough to operate on. We can't do this," I repeated, over and over. "We can't do this."

But that was not the issue. I had to face the real question. Should we do it? Did it need to be done? Deep down I already knew the answers. No matter how I tried to talk myself out of it, the bottom line was that the education George Wythe provided the leaders of America's founding needed to be re-established in modern America. No other institution I knew of was doing it well, if at all. A few had classics and some discussed mentoring in their literature, and certainly there were many times and places where great teachers inspired great learning, but no institution was delivering a full system including all of the Five Pillars of Statesmanship and Seven Keys of Great Teaching. I knew that as we continued the struggle to build George Wythe College, people would laugh at us—as they already were. They would criticize and attack what we were doing. We certainly could not afford to do it. But as hard as this clearly was going to be, nobody else was likely to do it. So I had to. Somebody else could do it better, I knew. Lots of people could do it better. But they were not doing it and it was so desperately needed.

I would do it, I decided—whatever it took, however long it took. Once I made the decision, I looked back up at the stars. I imagined a scene from the future.

The Speaker taps the gavel twice and calls for the vote in a room full of legislators. You sit back in your office chair, turn from the TV, close your eyes and ponder. At home, your family is gathered in the living room, also watching on television. Your married children and grandchildren tune in from their respective homes and places of business around the country. Nearly everyone is watching. The media have been discussing it for weeks, and are now giving a play-by-play account as Congress votes. Suddenly everything goes quiet.

A gasp goes through the House; you hear another ripple down the hall. You sit riveted, eyes wide open, unbelieving. How could this have happened?

You reach for the remote control, but before you can turn the television off, you hear a new voice. 'No.' The tone is gentle but firm. 'No,' repeats the voice. The camera pans the House chamber, and focuses on a young Congressman toward the back. He begins to speak. He is quiet, resolved, confident. His words are not rhetoric; they are common sense. They are timeless and speak deeply to our condition, to our struggles. You begin to nod your head. He speaks to our time, yet is rooted in history. His words are simple, and his suggestions direct. Other heads nod. He is brief, and ends with a motion.

The hall is filled with emotion. You feel it also. The floor stirs awkwardly. Then slowly, very slowly, another stands with courage and seconds the motion. And then another, and soon, another.

A final vote is taken. And while time stands still...a decision is reversed. The course of history changed by a few words.

Words like these take years to learn. Years of struggle and testing. Of right choices, and wrong choices followed by course corrections. Years of intense study, of prayer and devotion. Years of work in the military, in a sales position, in a struggling young home, in a managerial job, or in the risk years of launching a new business. But early lessons learned on the farm or in the boardroom are not forgotten. And the voices of mentors are remembered still.

Truth from the classroom and real life combine, and virtue, wisdom, diplomacy and courage converge to sway the course of history. Not just in the bodies of world power, but in our businesses, communities, schools, courtrooms, and homes.

So much depends on statesmanship. So much depends on education.

My mind shifted back to the present, and I realized that I was standing on my front porch, in a small town in America's heartland. I walked back into the house and told my wife Rachel I was going to stick it out. She said *we* would stick it out, whatever it took.

My vision of this young statesman strengthened my resolve. I knew that if we continued to build George Wythe College, men and women like him would get the education they must have in order to help lead us into a great future. I know that many parents, teachers, professors and administrators feel compelled by personal vision and mission to prepare the leaders of tomorrow with a great education today.

America will build a new Golden Age in the Twenty-first Century if we educate the next three generations with great classics and great mentors. We will prepare great leaders by bringing them face-to-face with greatness. If not, we will follow the path of other declining civilizations in history—from China, India, Greece and Rome to Spain, France and Britain.

It is our choice, and it is not a complex choice. It will be difficult to change the educational direction we have pursued for the last five decades. But it is time to clearly face the truth and choose wisely. Each of us should get started in our own homes and classrooms. We need not wait for anybody else. Our children must be offered an education up to par with their potential—and equal to the needs of the Twenty-first Century. We have the parents, the teachers, the educators and above all the students who are up to the task. It is time for a new generation to get a Thomas Jefferson Education.

100 Classics

100 Selections from the George Wythe College Classics List

Acton, *The History of Freedom*
John Adams, "Thoughts on Government"
Aquinas, "On Kingship"
Aristotle, *Nichomachean Ethics*
Aristotle, *Politics*
Aristotle, *Rhetoric*
Augustine, *The City of God*
Aurelius, *Meditations*
Austen, *Pride and Prejudice*
Austen, *Sense and Sensibility*
Bacon, *Novum Organum*
Bastiat, *The Law*
Bastiat, "What is Seen and Not Seen"
Benson, "The Proper Role of Government"
The Bible
Boethius, *The Consolation of Philosophy*
Bronte, *Wuthering Heights*
Bronte, *Jane Eyre*
Carson, *The American Tradition*
Capra, *The Tao of Physics*
Chesterton, *Orthodoxy*
Churchill, Collected Speeches
Cicero, *The Republic*
Cicero, *The Laws*
Clausewitz, *On War*
Confucius, *Analects*
The Constitution of the United States of America
Copernicus, *On the Revolutions of the Heavenly Spheres*
Covey, *The Seven Habits of Highly Effective People*

Dante, *The Divine Comedy*
The Declaration of Independence
DeFoe, *Robinson Crusoe*
Descartes, *A Discourse on Method*
Dickens, *A Tale of Two Cities*
Dickens, *Great Expectations*
Douglas, *Magnificent Obsession*
Durant, *A History of Civilization*
Einstein, *Relativity*
Emerson, Collected Essays
Euclid, *Elements*
Frank, *Alas Babylon*
Franklin, Letters and Writings
Freud, *Civilization and Its Discontents*
Galileo, *Two New Sciences*
Gibbon, *Decline and Fall of the Roman Empire*
Goethe, *Faust*
Hobbes, *Leviathan*
Homer, *The Iliad*
Homer, *The Odyssey*
Hugo, *Les Miserables*
Hume, *Essays Moral, Political and Literary*
Jefferson, Letters, Speeches and Writings
Keegan, *History of Warfare*
Kepler, *Epitome*
Martin Luther King, Jr., Collected Speeches
Kuhn, *The Structure of Scientific Revolutions*
Lavoisier, *Elements of Chemistry*
Lewis, *Mere Christianity*
Lewis, *The Screwtape Letters*
Lewis, *The Weight of Glory*
Lincoln, Collected Speeches
Locke, *Second Treatise of Government*
Machiavelli, *The Prince*
Madison, Hamilton and Jay, *The Federalist Papers*
Marx and Engels, *The Communist Manifesto*

More, *Utopia*
The Magna Charta
Mill, *On Liberty*
Milton, *Paradise Regained*
Mises, *Human Action*
The Monroe Doctrine
Montesquieu, *The Spirit of the Laws*
Newton, *Mathematical Principles*
Nichomachus, *Introduction to Arithmetic*
Nietzsche, *Beyond Good and Evil*
The Northwest Ordinance
Orwell, *1984*
Plato, Collected Works
Polybius, *Histories*
Potok, *The Chosen*
Plutarch, *Lives*
Ptolemy, *Algamest*
Shakespeare, *Collected Works*
Skousen, *The Five Thousand Year Leap*
Skousen, *The Majesty of God's Law*
Skousen, *The Making of America*
Smith, *The Wealth of Nations*
Solzhenitsyn, "A World Split Apart"
Solzhenitsyn, *The Gulag Archipelago*
Sophocles, *Oedipus Trilogy*
Stowe, *Uncle Tom's Cabin*
Sun Tzu, *The Art of War*
Thackeray, *Vanity Fair*
Thoreau, *Walden*
Tolstoy, *War and Peace*
Thucydides, *History of the Peloponnesian War*
Tocqueville, *Democracy in America*
Washington, Letters, Speeches and Writings
Weaver, *Mainspring of Human Progress*
Wister, *The Virginian*

Classics for Children and Youth

Two lists are presented here, one of classics to read to young children and the second for older youth to read and discuss with their mentors.

To Read to Young Children

Aesop's Fables
Andersen's Fairy Tales
Beauty and the Beast
The Bible
The Blind Men and the Elephant
"Casey at Bat"
Charlotte's Web
Chicken Little
A Christmas Carol
Cinderella
Dinotopia series
Dr. Seuss series
The Emperor's New Clothes
The Fourth Wise Man
The Gift of the Magi
The Giving Tree
"God Save the Flag"
Goldilocks and the Three Bears
The Goose That Laid the Golden Egg
Grimm's Fairy Tales
"The Highwayman"
Hansel and Gretel
Jack and the Beanstock
The Legend of Sleepy Hollow
"Lincoln, The Man of the People"
"Little Boy Blue"

The Little Engine that Could
The Little House on the Prairie series
The Little Red Hen
Little Red Riding Hood
McGuffey's Readers
Mother Goose's Nursery Rhymes
"Paul Revere's Ride"
Peter Pan
Peter Rabbit
The Pied Piper of Hamelin
Pinocchio
Pollyanna
The Princess and the Pea
Puss-in-Boots
Rapunzel
Riki Tiki Tavi
Rip Van Winkle
Robin Hood
Rumpelstiltskin
Rudyard Kipling "Just So" stories
Sleeping Beauty
The Song of Hiawatha
Snow White
Tales of the Arabian Nights
The Three Billy Goats Gruff
The Three Little Pigs
The Ugly Duckling
Tom Thumb
"'Twas the Night Before Christmas"
The Wind in the Willows
Winnie-the-Pooh series
The Wonderful Wizard of Oz

Classics For Youth

Alice in Wonderland

Animal Farm

Anne Frank: The Diary of a Young Girl

The *Anne of Green Gables* series

The Autobiography of Benjamin Franklin

"Battle Hymn of the Republic"

Ben Hur

The Bible

Brighty of the Grand Canyon

Black Beauty

The Black Stallion series

The Chronicles of Narnia series

The Collected Verse of Edgar A. Guest

"Concord Hymn"

A Connecticut Yankee in King Arthur's Court

The Constitution of the United States of America

David Copperfield

Davy Crockett Legends

The Declaration of Independence

The Deerslayer

Don Quixote

Dr. Jekyll and Mr. Hyde

The Dred Scott Decision

The Education of Henry Adams

Eight Cousins

Emily Post's Etiquette

Ender's Game

"In Flanders Fields"

Flatland

The Foundation series

Frankenstein

"The Gettysburg Address"

"Give Me Liberty or Give Me Death"

The Great Brain series

Gulliver's Travels

Hamilton's Mythology

Hamlet

Heidi
The Hiding Place
History Reborn
Huckleberry Finn
"I Have a Dream"
Ivanhoe
The Hobbit
Island of the Blue Dolphins
Joan of Arc (Twain)
Jo's Boys
A Journey to the Center of the Earth
Julius Caesar (Shakespeare)
The Jungle Book
King Arthur and the Round Table
Laddie
The Last of the Mohicans
"Let America Be America Again"
The Lincoln-Douglas Debates
The Little Britches series
Little Lord Fauntleroy
Little Men
Little Women
The Lonesome Gods
Lord of the Rings series
"The Man with the Hoe"
Mathematicians are People, Too (2 volumes)
Moby Dick
Narrative of the Life of Frederick Douglass
National Velvet
Noah Webster's Original 1828 Dictionary
North to Freedom
"O Captain! My Captain!"
"Old Ironsides"
Old Yeller
Oliver Twist
On Numbers

Paul Bunyan
The Phantom Tollbooth
"The Present Crisis"
"The Road Not Taken"
The Real Benjamin Franklin
The Real George Washington
The Real Thomas Jefferson
The Robe
Robinson Crusoe
Romeo and Juliet
The Sackett series
The Saxon Math series
The Secret Garden
Soldiers, Statesmen and Heroes
Sonnets of Shakespeare
Spiritual Lives of the Great Composers
Stuart Little
The Summer of the Monkeys
Swiss Family Robinson
Tom Sawyer
Treasure Island
The Trumpet of the Swans
"Ulysses"
The Voyages of Doctor Dolittle
The Walking Drum
White Fang
William Tell
Where the Red Fern Grows
The Yearling

Sample Discussion Questions

This appendix is not a thorough study guide, but rather a brief primer to help beginners start reading and discussing a few classics of literature for themselves. The list emphasizes literature because for most people this is the easiest place to start. It may be helpful to review the questions before reading the given book, take notes as you read and then discuss your answers or write about them after you finish each work. The terms "Bent, Broken, Whole, Healing" are discussed in Chapter Five and may be studied in more detail in *The Healing Power of Stories* by Daniel Taylor. I highly recommend that you read this fine book, a modern day classic, as you begin your study of the classics.

Austen, *Persuasion*

1. Many believe that *Persuasion* is Jane Austen's best book. Is it? Why or why not?
2. What do you learn about Jane Austen from her stories?
3. Is civility before marriage important? Do Austen's characters go too far?
4. Is civility after marriage important? Do Austen's characters go too far?
5. Should Anne have married the first time? Defend your answer.
6. Should Anne have married the second time? Defend your answer.
7. What factors should one weigh in determining whether or not to marry a certain person?

Austen, *Pride and Prejudice*

1. Compare the Victorian concept of courting with the modern idea of dating. Which is better? Why? List the pros and cons of each.

2. Why is Elizabeth so quick to trust Wickham and to distrust Darcy? Do you make similar mistakes?
3. Is "Pride and Prejudice" a good title for this book? Why or why not? What else might it be titled?
4. Do manners correspond with morals in this book? What about in real life?
5. Compare the marriage relationships of the Bennets, Collins, Gardners and Phillips. Discuss the pros and cons of each.
6. Is the Elizabeth/Darcy marriage at the end a better marriage than the others? Why or why not?
7. More importantly, is it an ideal marriage? Why or why not?
8. Does Austen give an accurate and thorough portrayal of men? Why or why not?

Austen, *Sense and Sensibility*

1. Are core beliefs shown by actions? Why or why not?
2. Based on her actions, what were Elinor's core beliefs?
3. Based on her actions, what were Marianne's core beliefs?
4. Based on his actions, what were Willoughby's core beliefs?
5. Based on his actions, what were Edward's core beliefs?
6. Was Edward dishonest?
7. Pick two minor characters (not listed above) and analyze their character traits.

Bronte, *Jane Eyre*

1. What is Jane Eyre's philosophy of God?
2. Is there a reason why Rochester sometimes uses the name Jane and sometimes uses the name Janet?
3. What is St. John's philosophy of love and marriage? Rochester's? Jane's? Yours?
4. Is Jane Eyre's character strong or weak? Discuss.
5. Under the circumstances, would it have been okay for Jane to just marry Rochester even though he was already married?
6. Why is marriage so important? What are the clear rules which govern it?

7. How does marriage impact society?
8. Do you think Jane should have gone back to Rochester? Why or why not?
9. Did Rochester change by the end of the book? How?
10. Do you find any symbolism in Rochester's blindness?
11. In what ways are you like Jane? Rochester? St. John?

Bronte, *Wuthering Heights*

1. This book is considered by many the greatest English novel ever written. Why might this be so?
2. How accurate is this as a portrayal of English society?
3. Do the people in this book get the partners they deserve?
4. Why does Catherine marry Edgar?
5. Why does Catherine want both Edgar and Heathcliff to suffer?
6. What is Heathcliff's goal in life? Does he achieve it?
7. Contrast Joseph and Nelly.
8. Pick at least six characters and show how each of them is a foil, or opposite, of Heathcliff.
9. Describe the difference between Edgar's and Heathcliff's "love."
10. Could any two of the characters have had a happy marriage? Who are they? Defend your answer.
11. Does Cathy heal the story? Explain.
12. Does Hareton? Explain.
13. Does Heathcliff change? Defend your answer.

Dickens, *Great Expectations*

1. In the first few chapters of the book, how is Pip like you? How is he different? How does this change?
2. Was it right for Pip to reject Magwitch's money? Why or why not?
3. Separate from the question above, did Pip reject the money for the right reason?
4. Compare Pip's life to The Inner Ring concept from C.S. Lewis' *The Weight of Glory*. Be specific.

5. How did Pip's changed "expectations" change his life? How do similar circumstances affect you?
6. Do money and status corrupt? Under what circumstances? Why?
7. What are your great expectations? What rules do you need to maintain while you seek them?

Dickens, *A Tale of Two Cities*

1. Is Sidney Carton a Christ figure? Elaborate.
2. How was the French Revolution different from the American Revolution?
3. Who is your favorite character in the book? Why?
4. What other books of literature have you read that deal with the French Revolution? Compare them with this book.
5. Analyze Madame Defarge. What characteristics does she personify?
6. Is this a book about history, or symbols, or politics, or passion? Defend your answer.
7. What is the main message of this story?
8. How should it be applied in your personal life? In the modern world?

Emerson, *Essays*

1. As you read, make the following lists:
   A. Statements you agree with.
   B. Statements you disagree with.
   C. Statements which apply to our current society.
2. Pick the ten most important items from the above lists and explain your reasons for agreeing or disagreeing.

Frank, *Alas Babylon*

1. What things changed suddenly with the bomb? What would change in your life in a similar catastrophe?
2. Was the new society Randy founded successful? Why or why not?

3. Should Ben have killed the dog? Should Randy have killed the highwaymen? (Compare the Virginian and Trampas.)
4. What things surprised you about the way they lived?
5. What things would you need to do to prepare for similar circumstances?
6. What would you do differently?

Goulding, *The Lord of the Flies*

1. Was Simon a true prophet type? Why or why not?
2. Was Piggy a true intellectual type? Why or why not?
3. Was Ralph a true statesman type? Why or why not?
4. Was Jack a true tyrant type? Why or why not?
5. Was the relation between the leaders and the masses (the "littluns") an accurate portrayal of real governments and societies? Why or why not?
6. Discuss the symbolism of the conch.
7. What is required to maintain civilization?
8. Discuss the symbolism of the soldier who rescues the boys at the end. Be specific.
9. Was the book an accurate type of the world?
10. How do you think this book should be healed?
11. If one of your children were on the plane, what would you want them to do differently? What preparation do they need in order to effectively do it?

Hawthorne, *The Scarlet Letter*

1. Who were the "healers" in this book?
2. Discuss Chillingsworth as a healer.
3. Discuss Dimsdale as a leader.
4. Discuss Hester's strengths/weaknesses.
5. Discuss the strengths/weaknesses of Puritanical society.
6. How is that society different from our own? Be specific.
7. How is that society different from the ideal society? Be specific.
8. Discuss Pearl as a symbol.

Hugo, *Les Miserables*

1. Is this book bent, broken, whole, or healing?
2. What is Jean Valjean looking for in this story, and does he find it?
3. Why does Victor Hugo bring Thenardier back in the end of the book?
4. Was the Bishop right to give Valjean the rest of the silver and let him go free? Why or why not?
5. If Jean Valjean had told Marius that he was the man who saved him, how do you think Marius would have reacted? What was the author's purpose here?
6. Is there a comparison between Jean Valjean and the sewer?
7. Some have said that, next to the scriptures, this is the best book ever written. Why do you think they would say this? Be specific.
8. Using specific references to the book, discuss the atonement.
9. How does Javert personify justice?
10. How does Valjean personify mercy?
11. How are justice and mercy reconciled in *Les Miserables*?
12. Using comparison and contrast, discuss good parenting as exemplified by characters in *Les Miserables*.
13. Is "Les Miserables" a good title for this book? Discuss its symbolism and meaning, and suggest and defend other possible titles.
14. Are Hugo's main characters static or do they change? Defend your answer for each.
15. List at least nine crises that Valjean faces. How does he react to each, and with which does he progress or regress?
16. Out of all his trials, which was Valjean's ultimate test? Did he pass?
17. Hugo dedicates a relatively large space to descriptions of buildings, clothes, how people look, etc. Explain how these symbols support the story.

Lewis, *The Weight of Glory*

1. Make a list of the key ideas you identify in each chapter.
2. What are you doing about the three enemies of success in your life?
3. What inner rings are there in your life?
4. What do you need to do to be a master craftsman?
5. From the chapter on Membership: What things in life should be public? Private? Make a list and defend it.
6. As you read, make the following lists:
   A. Things you agree with.
   B. Things you disagree with.
   C. Things you want to incorporate into your life.
   D. Things you need to incorporate into your life.

Orwell, *1984*

1. This is a sick story. Is it healthier or sicker than our modern society? Explain your answer.
2. Make a list of specific parallels between *1984* and our society. Also a list of specific differences.
3. What is your overall opinion of the result of these two lists?
4. Show how the State in *1984* is like a church, a religion.
5. Is that good or bad? Why?
6. Find and clip at least five current newspaper articles with examples of "newspeak."
7. Can such a change to society happen to ours? What could make it happen, or what could stop it?

Potok, *The Chosen*

1. Is this a bent, broken, whole or healing story? Why?
2. What is the theme of this book? Silence, fathers, relationships, education, Jewish culture, the way God speaks to us, or something else?
3. Are there any good things about using silence the way Danny's father did in raising children?

4. Some Christian analysts feel that Danny personifies Jewish culture and Reuven in many ways personifies Christian culture. Do you see any truth in this analysis? Why or why not?
5. How is the history of Judaism's relationship to God similar to Danny's relationship with his father?
6. What did you learn about educational methods and systems from this book? Which can you apply?
7. Analyze Reuven's and Danny's fathers as prototypes in the role of father. List and discuss the pros and cons of each.
8. Was Danny's final choice right?
9. Research and explain the history of Chaim Potok.
10. Compare and contrast Reuven's and Danny's views with those of Portia and Shylock in *The Merchant of Venice*.

Shakespeare, *Henry V*

1. Is Henry V the ideal Christian King or a bloody conqueror? Defend your answer.
2. Compare Henry V to Napoleon. Who was better for Europe? Defend your answer.
3. Compare Henry V and the French King. Which is the better ruler? Which would you rather have as a king? Explain your answers.
4. Are kings to blame for war? What about peace? What are kings responsible for?
5. Answer Question 4 again, but insert the word "government" wherever it says "king."
6. How do you feel about Henry's wooing of Katherine? Is he a good, gentle suitor or a tyrant? Are his wooing and conquering techniques similar or different?
7. In Katherine's shoes, what would you do? Explain your answer.
8. List four characters not listed here and discuss them, their contributions, ideas, reasons for their actions, etc.

Shakespeare, *King John*

1. Is Shakespeare's *King John* historically accurate? Research and discuss.
2. Why are infidelity and war so closely related?
3. Research the War of the Roses and discuss how this helped you understand this play.
4. From your research, diagram the family of Henry II and discuss whether or not King John is the rightful heir to the throne.
5. Why is infidelity blamed mostly on the women? Should it be?
6. Should Hurbert have killed Arthur?
7. Discuss John's strengths/weaknesses.

Shakespeare, *The Merchant of Venice*

1. Justice versus Mercy: What are the rules and how does it work? (Compare to *Les Miserables*)
2. Compare Christianity to Judaism; what are the central beliefs and behaviors of each in this play? Based on your research, how accurate is Shakespeare's stereotypes of these cultures?
3. On what points is Shylock right?
4. On what points is Portia wrong?
5. Venice was at that time what America is today to our world: the leading world power—economically, politically and socially. How is our culture like that of the Venice described in the play?
6. Do Portia and her friends really believe in mercy? Discuss by analyzing their use of mercy toward Shylock.

Shakespeare, *Romeo and Juliet*

1. Why is this one of the most popular love stories of all time?
2. Is deception ever right? Defend your answer.
3. Shakespeare portrays several types of "love." What are they? Which are right? What is real love?

4. Which men in the play would have been the best choices as spouses? List at least four possibilities and show their strengths and weaknesses.
5. What were Juliet's strengths/weaknesses? List and discuss.
6. What were Romeo's strengths/weaknesses? List and discuss.
7. What were Friar Lawrence's strengths/weaknesses? List and discuss.
8. Was Romeo really in love? Defend your answer.
9. Does love just "happen" to you; and must you uncontrollably follow it? Explain.
10. Discuss trusting God as the central theme of this play. ("curse you, stars").

Shakespeare, *The Taming of the Shrew*

1. Was there a good marriage in this play? Which one(s)? Defend your answer.
2. Is Baptista a good father?
3. Is Katherine really a shrew, or does she just treat men as they deserve?
4. What are Petruchio's strengths/weaknesses? List and discuss.
5. What are Petruchio's motivations?
6. When should anger be fought with flattery?
7. When should anger be fought with anger?
8. When should anger be fought with force?
9. Is Petruchio a hero or an abuser? Discuss.
10. Compare this story to *All's Well That Ends Well*.

Shakespeare, *The Tempest*

1. Compare *The Tempest* to *Lord of the Flies*. Be specific.
2. Discuss repentance and reconciliation as a central theme of *The Tempest*.
3. Discuss torment and suffering as a central theme of *The Tempest*.
4. Discuss purification through suffering as a central theme of *The Tempest*.

5. How is this play an allegory to life? Be specific.
6. List at least five personality types represented. Discuss.
7. Are there more than five? What are they?
8. Discuss nature vs. society as a central theme.
9. Discuss illusion vs. reality as a central theme.
10. Compare the various personality types in *The Tempest* to those in *War and Peace*. Be specific.
11. Discuss which parts seem to be Shakespeare speaking through Prospero.

Stowe, *Uncle Tom's Cabin*

1. Is Uncle Tom a Christ archetype? Compare him to Sydney Carton from *A Tale of Two Cities*.
2. On a personal level, Legree is clearly the worst slave master. On a national level, who is the most likely to influence society to keep slavery as an institution: Legree, the Shelbys or St. Clare? Defend your answer.
3. Besides Tom, who were the heroes of the book? Why?
4. Describe the symbolism of the title: "Uncle Tom's Cabin." What was it about his cabin that made it central?
5. Was the main theme of the book: Slavery is evil? No fence sitters? Society brings out the best in people? You can enslave the body, but you can't enslave the soul? Love can change people? Faith is power? Faith is doing what is right no matter the circumstance? Something else? Defend your answer.
6. Take one or more of the themes in Question 5 and develop.
7. What is real Christianity? Use the book to support your answer.
8. Why is the phrase "Uncle Tom" often used as a negative in the modern black community?

Thackeray, *Vanity Fair*

1. As you read, make a list of Becky Sharp's positive character traits.

2. Also make a list of negative character traits.
3. Did Becky have a fatal flaw which led to the rest of her problems? Discuss.
4. Is there a hero in this story? Make a list of five possible heroes/heroines. Discuss why each is a hero/heroine and why he/she falls short.
5. Make a list of lessons we should learn from this book and apply in our modern world.

Thoreau, *Walden*

1. As you read, make the following lists:
   A. Everything about modern society which is true.
   B. Everything about modern society which is false.
   C. Each idea you never thought of before.
   D. Each idea you would like to apply to your life.
2. Compare *Walden* to Emerson's *Essays*. Where do the two of them disagree?
3. Discuss any other lesson(s) you learned.

Tolstoy, *War and Peace*

1. Do fate or choices determine the path of people's lives? Or both? Or something else?
2. Use specific examples and characters to support or refute the following statements: "Wars go on around us, as do many other events. The important thing is not what happens to us but how we respond."
3. List five characters who respond positively and five who respond negatively. Discuss the differences between the two lists; why do some choose good and some evil? (Compare to Shakespeare's *The Tempest*)
4. Who was the hero of this book? Defend your answer.
5. What are the key lessons of this book?
6. Make a list of all the sources Pierre looks to for the truth. Did he miss any? Which is the best?

Wister, *The Virginian*

1. How does the Virginian personify the American Tradition? (Compare to Carson's *The American Tradition*)
2. Compare the pros and cons of Boston society versus Western society. Which is better?
3. Should the Virginian have taken part in the hanging? Was it murder or law enforcement? What makes the difference? (Compare to Frank's *Alas Babylon*)
4. Should the Virginian have fought Trampas? What should people do in a society with no strong law enforcement?
5. Where does law come from? (Compare to Benson's "The Proper Role of Government")

Where to Find the Classics

In addition to public and university libraries, the classics are available in many used book stores and can often be purchased from people who have them in their homes, but haven't used them. These methods of obtaining the classics can save you a significant amount of money. Many classics are available electronically, which is valuable for research and comparison and may be helpful in writing about the classics, but is not recommended for actual reading; books are much more user friendly and foster better thinking and pondering. A number of publishers print or distribute classics, including the following:

Bantam Classics (Bantam Books)
Classic Books
Dover Classics (Dover Publications, many titles available for
    under $2)
Everyman's Library
Foundation for Economic Education
George Wythe College Bookstore
The Great Books of the Western World (Britannica)
Great Books in Philosophy series (Prometheus Books)
The Great Ideas (Britannica)
Great Minds series (Prometheus Books)
The Harvard Classics (Collier)
The Hirsch Core Knowledge series (Doubleday)
The Institute for Excellence in Writing
The Junior Classics series (Collier)
Kimber Principle-Centered Curriculum
The Modern Library of the World's Best Books (Random House)
The National Center for Constitutional Studies
The Noah Plan (Foundation for American Christian Education)
Penguin Classics (Penguin Books)

Saxon Math
Signet Classics (Penguin Books)
Touchstone Books (Simon and Schuster)
Wordsworth Classics of World Literature
World's Classics (Oxford University Press)

Recommended Readings

Adler, *Reforming American Education*
Bacon, *Novum Organum*
Barton, *What Happened in Education?*
Barzun, *Teacher in America*
Bennett, *The Book of Virtues*
Bloom, A., *The Closing of the American Mind*
Bloom, H., *The Western Canon*
Blumenfeld, *How to Tutor*
Blumenfeld, *The New Illiterates*
Bunting, *An Education for Our Time*
Colfax, *Home Schooling for Excellence*
Covey, *First Things First*
Dewey, *The School and Society*
Emerson, "The American Scholar"
Gardner, *Multiple Intelligences*
Gardner, *The Unschooled Mind*
Gatto, *Dumbing Us Down*
Gatto, *The Exhausted School*
Glasser, *The Quality School*
Harward, *A Market Approach to Education*
Hirsch, *Cultural Literacy*
Hirsch, et al., *The Dictionary of Cultural Literacy*
Holt, *How Children Fail*
Holt, *How Children Learn*
Hutchins, *The Higher Learning in America*
Kirk, *Redeeming the Times*
Lewis, *The Abolition of Man*
Mason, *The Original Home School Series* (6 vol.)
Montessori, all writings
Nash, *The Closing of the American Heart*
Noebel, *Understanding the Times*

Ortega y Gasset, *Mission of the University*
Perelman, *School's Out*
Pudewa, all writings
Smith, *Killing the Spirit*
Strauss and Howe, *The Fourth Turning*
Swanson, *The Education of James Madison*
Taylor, *The Healing Power of Stories*
Toffler, *Futureshock*
Van Doren, *Liberal Education*

Putting Thomas Jefferson Education to Work

"Anything worth doing well is worth doing poorly—at first."

—Ray Congdon

"Ready, fire, aim."

—Tom Peters

How to Get Started: Months 1-2

This appendix is for beginners, for those who aren't sure how to get started. If you are already using the TJEd model, or if you are a real self-starter with little need for structure and outside direction, you probably don't need this appendix; instead, review Chapters Four and Six and start incorporating all the keys to great mentoring and teaching. If you are an administrator, review Chapter Seven.

If, on the other hand, you are just starting and need help or have tried to start but just couldn't seem to make it work, then read on.

If you are going to follow this system, follow it closely. Do one step at a time; that is, read one step, then finish it before moving on to the next step.

Step One: Forget the Kids

Just keep them doing whatever they've been doing until now. Don't add or change anything in your regular homeschool or classroom. Focus on you. You must become a better teacher, a mentor, before you change your teaching and mentoring.

Step Two: Read a Classic

Read one of the following this week:

The Chosen by Chaim Potok
Little Britches by Ralph Moody
Laddie by Jeanne Stratton-Porter
Anne of Green Gables by L.M. Montgomery
The Lonesome Gods by Louis L'Amour

Just pick one, the one that sounds most interesting, and read it.

Step Three: Read Three More Classics

Read one of the following classics each week for the rest of the month (by the end of the month you should have read four of the five):

The Chosen by Chaim Potok
Little Britches by Ralph Moody
Laddie by Jeanne Stratton-Porter
Anne of Green Gables by L.M. Montgomery
The Lonesome Gods by Louis L'Amour

Step Four: Read and Annotate a Classic

Complete the following within one week:

A. Read once through the *Declaration of Independence*.
B. Read it again, this time looking up every unclear word in a dictionary. Write down each definition.
C. Read it again and write down ten ideas that are interesting to you from the reading.
D. Sit down with at least two different people and explain your ten ideas to them. Give them a copy of the *Declaration* so that you can refer to specific items during your explanation.

Step Five: Annotate Two More Classics

Read two of the following classics by the end of the month:

Pride and Prejudice by Jane Austen
A Tale of Two Cities by Charles Dickens
The Merchant of Venice by William Shakespeare
Walden by Henry David Thoreau

After reading each, complete the following:

A. Answer the questions in Appendix C, in writing, for each book.
B. Sit down with at least one person and discuss your answers and other thoughts about each book.

Steps 1-5 should be completed within 60 days; if it takes longer, do not go on to Step 6 until Steps 1-5 are completed.

How to Get Your Students Started: Months 3-4

Once you have completed Steps 1-5, you are prepared to help your students get started. Of course, you will still be doing more work than they are for at least the first year. Make sure that you refer to the discussion on the Phases of Learning to determine how to proceed with your children/students. If the student is in Core Phase or early Love of Learning, just keep studying classics yourself until she is ready for these additional steps. Use this time to create a TJEd environment in your home or classroom.

Please complete each step before reading the next.

Step Six: Have the Student(s) Read a Classic

A. Assign the student(s) to read one of the following:

The Chosen by Chaim Potok
Little Britches by Ralph Moody
Laddie by Jeanne Stratton-Porter
Anne of Green Gables by L.M. Montgomery
The Lonesome Gods by Louis L'Amour

B. Set a time to discuss this reading.
C. Re-read the classic yourself and take lots of notes.
D. Have the discussion; be patient and let the student(s) open up.

Step Seven: Have a Group Discussion.

Arrange a group discussion with at least 8 people, including yourself and your student, who all do the following:

A. Read one of the following (everyone must read the same book):

The Chosen by Chaim Potok
Little Britches by Ralph Moody
Laddie by Jeanne Stratton-Porter
Anne of Green Gables by L.M. Montgomery
The Lonesome Gods by Louis L'Amour

B. Set a time to discuss this reading.
C. Re-read the classic yourself and take lots of notes. Guide the discussion using the methods discussed in Chapter Six.
D. Have the discussion; be patient and let the students open up.

Step Eight: Repeat Step Seven

Use a different book from the list; have the same people attend the group discussion.

The First Year: A Weekly, Monthly and Annual Plan

Step Nine: Plan the Next 6 Months

A. Create a Weekly Schedule. With your student(s), make a plan for weekly studies including:
   1) Your daily study hours.
   2) Student daily study hours.
   3) Their daily assignment to write what they have learned.
   4) Daily or at least weekly Discussion Time to discuss what they have learned (in homeschool, both parents should be involved in this if possible).

B. Create a Schedule for this Month. With your students, make a plan for the following:
   1) Classics they will study. Discussion time (Choose from works on Appendix B at first, later move to works on Appendix A).
   2) Classics you will study. You should read student classics, plus get ahead on your own.
   3) Other studies. Discussion time.
   4) Field trips, simulations, other activities, and discussion times about each.
   5) Group discussions (one or two per month to begin with), the topics, and who will be involved. You may need to meet and schedule separately with all those involved in your Group Discussions.
   6) Visiting lectures (one or two per month to start, or a mini-class with multiple lectures by one teacher).

C. Schedule a time to meet each month to reorganize your Weekly Schedule if needed and to plan your Month Schedule. For most people, the best method is a set time, such as 9 a.m. every First Tuesday or 6 p.m. every Last Sunday. Plan your meeting times for the next six months and write all six on your calendar.

You may proceed with Step 10 before completing Step 9.

Step 10: Increase the Difficulty

After six months of classics study, depending on each teacher's and student's progress, you should begin increasing the difficulty of your readings. Over time, work up to the most challenging classics. Discussions and planning should follow the same general format at all levels.

Notes

Chapter One

1   See *The Two Towers* by J.R.R. Tolkien. The reference is also an allusion to the Twin Towers which fell under terrorist attack on September 11, 2001.

Chapter Two

2   Jacques Barzun. 1945. *Teacher in America*. Indianapolis: Liberty Fund. 7-9. As Dr. Barzun warned as early as 1945: "...Americans believe in Education, because they pay large sums to yield results. At this point one is bound to ask: 'What results do you expect?' The replies are staggering. Apparently Education is to do everything that the rest of the world leaves undone. Recall the furore over American History. Under new and better management that subject was to produce patriots—nothing less. An influential critic, head of a large university, wants education to generate a classless society; another asks that education root out racial intolerance (in the third or the ninth grade, I wonder?); still another requires that college courses be designed to improve labor relations. One man, otherwise sane, thinks the solution of the housing problem has bogged down—in the schools; and another proposes to make the future house holders happy married couples—through the schools.... Then there are hundreds of specialists in the endless 'vocations' who want Education to turn out practised engineers, affable hotelkeepers, and finished literary artists....But to say this is to show up the folly of perpetually confusing Education with the work of the schools; the folly of believing against all evidence that by taking boys and girls for a few hours each day between the ages of seven and twenty-one, our teachers can 'turn out' all the human products that we like to fancy when we are disgusted with ourselves and our neighbors."

3   Ibid. 4-6.

4   William Shakespeare. *Hamlet*. Act I, Scene iii.

5   MaryAnn Johnson. 1997. "Can a Liberal Arts Education Get Me a Job?" *The Statesman*. Cedar City: George Wythe College. 3.1.2.

6   Ibid.

7   Op. Cit. Barzun, xix.

8   Mortimer J. Adler. 1977. *Reforming Education: The Opening of the American Mind*. New York: Collier. 233. He continues: "They have turned the whole nation—so far as education is concerned—into a kindergarten. It must all

be fun. It must all be entertaining. Adult learning must be made as effortless as possible—painless, devoid of oppressive burdens and of irksome tasks. Adult men and women, because they are adult, can be expected to suffer pains of all sorts in the course of their daily occupations, whether domestic or commercial. We do not try to deny the fact that taking care of a household or holding down a job is necessarily burdensome, but we somehow still believe that the goods to be attained, the worldly goods of wealth and comfort, are worth the effort. In any case, we know they cannot be obtained without effort. But we try to shut our eyes to the fact that improving one's mind or enlarging one's spirit is, if anything, more difficult than solving the problems of subsistence..."

Chapter Three

9 Adapted from a story "The Little Boy"; author unknown, although the story is often attributed to Helen Buckley.

10 For an excellent study of education in history, review passages on education from Will Durant. *The History of Civilization*. New York: MJF Books.

11 I couldn't find an original source for this quote. It is credited to Lincoln in a number of places, so I give him credit for it though I couldn't find it in his writings.

12 See Thomas Jefferson. Albert Ellery Bergh, ed. 1907. *The Writings of Thomas Jefferson*. The Thomas Jefferson Memorial Association. 13.396.

13 For example, John Taylor Gatto lists the seven lessons of public schooling as: 1) confusion, 2) class position, 3) indifference, 4) emotional dependency, 5) intellectual dependency, 6) provisional self-esteem, and 7) one can't hide. For a more complete discussion, see his book: John Taylor Gattto. 1992. *Dumbing Us Down: The Hidden Curriculum of Compulsory Schooling*. Philadelphia: New Society Publishers.

14 J. Bottum. "Deciding to Home School." *The Weekly Standard*. February 7, 2000.

15 William R. Mattox, Jr. "Hidden Virtues in Home Schooling," *USA Today*. February 3, 1999.

Chapter Four

16 Theodore C. Sorensen. 1965. *Kennedy*. New York: Harper & Row, Publishers. 384.

17 Fawn M. Brodie. 1974. *Thomas Jefferson: An Intimate History*. New York: W. W. Norton & Company, Inc. 61.

18 Allan Bloom. 1987. *The Closing of the American Mind*. New York: Simon and Schuster. 59-60.

19 Thanks to Tiffany Rhoades Earl for coining this phrase.

20 See the writings of Samuel Blumenfeld and John Holt.

Chapter Five

21 Op. Cit. Bloom, 57-59. He continues: "Almost everyone in the middle class has a college degree, and most have an advanced degree of some kind. Those of us who can look back to the humble stations of our parents or grandparents, who never saw the inside of an institution of higher learning, can have cause for self-congratulation. But...the impression that our general populace is better educated depends on an ambiguity in the meaning of the word education, or a fudging of the distinction between liberal and technical education. A highly trained computer specialist need not have had any more learning about morals, politics or religion than the most ignorant of persons. All to the contrary, his narrow education, with the prejudices and the pride accompanying it, and its literature which comes to be and passes away in a day and uncritically accepts the premises of current wisdom, can cut him off from the liberal learning that simpler folk used to absorb from a variety of traditional sources."

22 Ibid. 60.

23 Thucydides, *History of the Peloponnesian War*. 1,1.84. Quoted from: Josiah Bunting III. 1998. *An Education For Our Time*. Washington DC: Regnery.

24 See C. S. Lewis. 1982. *The Screwtape Letters*. London: Bantam Books. 73-75.

25 See Daniel Taylor. 1996. *The Healing Power of Stories: Creating Yourself Through the Stories of Your Life*. New York: Doubleday.

Chapter Six

26 Andy Groft. 2000. George Wythe College Course handout.

27 Troy Henke. 2000. George Wythe College course handout.

28 Op. Cit. Barzun, 195-96. Note that Barzun provides a valuable commentary on teaching many of these same subjects. I was surprised when I read his book to see how similar our conclusions are, but perhaps an education in the classics does, as Adler argues, lead to the same answers—certainly it should illuminate true principles.

29 Henry David Thoreau. 1995. *Walden; Or, Life in the Woods*. New York: Dover Publications. 34.

Chapter Seven

30 Herbert J. Walberg. "The Cost of a Proficient Student" *The Weekly Standard*, December 23, 2002, 41. Hoover Institution. (1998 statistics).

31 *Outcomes of Learning: Results from the 2000 Program for International Student Assessment of 15-Year-Olds in Reading, Mathematics, and Science Literacy.* NCES' PISA Web site at http://nces.ed.gov/surveys/pisa. National Center for Education Statistics, Institute of Educational Sciences, U.S. Department of Education. (2000 statistics).

32 Op Cit. Walberg.

Chapter Eight

33 Thanks to Page Smith for these quotes. See Page Smith. 1990. *Killing the Spirit: Higher Education in America.* New York: Penguin.

34 Op. Cit. Smith, 54.

35 Ibid. 132.

36 George Wythe College Mission Statement.

Chapter Nine

37 For a more complete analysis of these trends, see: Robert Reich. 1991. *The Work of Nations: Preparing Ourselves for Twenty-first Century Capitalism.* New York: Alfred A. Knopf; Paul Kennedy. 1993. *Preparing for the Twenty-first Century.* New York: Random House; Alvin Toffler. 1991. *PowerShift: Knowledge, Wealth, and Violence at the Edge of the Twenty-first Century.* New York: Bantam Books; Peter Drucker. 1993. *Post-Capitalist Society.* New York: HarperBusiness; Harry S. Dent. 1998. *The Roaring 2000s.* New York: Simon and Schuster.

38 Thanks to John Taylor Gatto for pointing these out. In preparation for the Twenty-first Century, various faculties at Harvard's Graduate Division issued advice to students targeting specific skills thought to be in demand for the job market of the future. Encountering a stack of these advisories on a visit to Cambridge, John Taylor Gatto summarized these into ten points.

39 Report of the 1993 Strategic Planning Committee on Undergraduate Education, Princeton University.

40 Op. Cit. Johnson.

Chapter Ten

41 Quoted in W. David Stedman and LaVaughn G. Lewis, eds.1987. *Our Ageless Constitution.* Bicentennial Edition. Asheboro, North Carolina: W. David Stedman Associates. 20.

42 Ibid. p. 267.

43 Ibid. Note that the original source of this quote is no longer extant; it is attributed to Alexander Tytler.

Leadership Education Resources

TJEd.org

The official website of Thomas Jefferson Education.

Every person has inner genius. Thomas Jefferson Education consists of helping each student discover, develop and polish her genius. This is the essence and very definition of great education.

TJEd.org provides resources to help you apply the 7 Keys of Great Teaching to ignite a life-long passion for learning in you and your kids. And check out **This Week in History**, a daily cross-curricular resource to help you inspire them and bring them face-to-face with greatness.

OTHER WORKS BY OLIVER DEMILLE

Leadership Education: The Phases of Learning

(with Rachel DeMille)

This volume continues the Leadership Education Library with dedicated sections – including extremely valuable how-to with examples and resources – for each of the Phases of Learning: Core, Love of Learning, Transition to Scholar, Scholar and Depth. In addition, this book illuminates the adult phases of Mission and Impact, with a special Coda on Grandparenting. If you want to implement Leadership Education in your home, school, business or personal life, you will find this an invaluable tool. This inspirational book is considered by many to be the DeMille's best work.

Thomas Jefferson Education for Teens

(with Shanon Brooks)

This addition to the TJEd library is written to youth and adults wanting to accomplish a successful Scholar Phase–academics, personal development and mission preparation.

It includes: "How to find the 'Real You'"; The Teen-100 List; How to study the classic; How to make the most of your mentor; Sample Simulations; ...plus lots more!

A Thomas Jefferson Education Home Companion

(with Rachel DeMille and Diann Jeppson)

This handy sequel has practical suggestions for helping children progress toward and succeed in scholar phase, including adult skills acquisition, how to conduct a successful family reading time, mentoring tips, club organization helps, how to create a "Momschool," etc.

The Student Whisperer

(with Tiffany Earl)

This book is designed to help you become a great mentor—a true Student Whisperer and leader at the highest level. It will also help you work effectively with such mentors as you pursue your goals and life mission. This book is part deep teaching of the vital principles of great Leadership Education, part self-help workshop, part example through parables, and part exploration of the great ideas that make mentoring and quality learning most effective at all ages.

AUDIOS

The Seven Keys of Great Teaching

"The 7 Keys of Great Teaching" is an mp3 audio download of a two-hour presentation delivered before a live audience by Oliver DeMille. One of the most popular and widely shared of our audios, this inspiring lecture covers the basics of TJEd:

- The 3 Types of Education
- The 4 Phases of Learning
- The 7 Keys of Great Teaching

Engaging, entertaining and informative, "The 7 Keys of Great Teaching" is an excellent first tool for sharing the principles and overview of Leadership Education with family, friends, educational advisers, mentors, spouses, students, etc.

Core and Love of Learning Seminar Highlights

"Core and Love of Learning: A Recipe for Success" is a 5-hour audio series consisting of highlights from a two-day seminar presented by Oliver and Rachel DeMille in 2007. This mp3 download will help you develop and expand your vision of how the TJEd model can work in your home. Oliver and Rachel's spontaneous, candid, intimate, touching, humorous and profound commentary on Leadership Education in the home includes:

- Organizing Space in your home to support Thomas Jefferson Education
- What to simplify and what to beef up
- What to say "No" to, and when to say "Yes"
- Music and other lessons and how to best integrate them
- Organizing a big family with students at different ages and Phases
- Separating discipline from academics
- Using outside activities without letting them take over

The Four Lost American Ideals

In the hour-long recorded lecture, "The Four Lost American Ideals" Oliver DeMille draws from intensive study of the Founding generation to identify five defining ideals of Americanism: 1) Freedom, 2) Georgics, 3) Providence, 4) Liber and 5) Public Virtue. Although the first, Freedom, has not yet been fully lost, it is steadily declining because of the loss of the other four. These four ideals permeated early American society but have largely been forgotten.

For these and other resources, visit http://tjed.org/

Connect with Thomas Jefferson Education on Facebook, Twitter and YouTube!

For additional resources for adult education, leadership and professional development, visit:

- The official site of Oliver DeMille at http://OliverDeMille.com
- The Center for Social Leadership at http://thesocialleader.com

About the Author

Oliver DeMille is the author of *A Thomas Jefferson Education, FreedomShift* and other books, articles and audios on education and freedom.

Oliver is a popular keynote speaker, writer and business consultant. He is married to the former Rachel Pinegar. They have eight children.

Connect with Oliver on Facebook, Twitter and at www.OliverDeMille.com.